FATAL FLAWS

HANK HANEGRAAFF

THOMAS NELSON
Since 1798

NASHVILLE   DALLAS   MEXICO CITY   RIO DE JANEIRO   BEIJING

FATAL FLAWS

Published in Nashville, Tennessee, by Thomas Nelson. Thomas Nelson is a registered trademark of Thomas Nelson, Inc.

Thomas Nelson, Inc. titles may be purchased in bulk for educational, business, fund-raising, or sales promotional use. For information, please e-mail SpecialMarkets@ThomasNelson.com.

Scripture quotations used in this book are from the Holy Bible, New International Version, copyright © 1973, 1978, 1984 by International Bible Society. Used by permission of Zondervan Publishing House.

Library of Congress Cataloging-in-Publication Data

Hanegraaff, Hank.
Fatal flaws / Hank Hanegraaff
p. cm.
Includes bibliographical references.
ISBN 978-0-8499-1795-0
ISBN 978-0-8499-1519-2 (trade paper)
1. Evolution (Biology)—Religious aspects—Christianity.
2. Darwin, Charles, 1809–1882. I. Title.
BT712.H363   2003

231.7'652–dc21   2003007933
CIP

Printed in the United States of America
07 08 09 10 11 RRD 5 4 3 2 1

To my wife, Kathy, "a woman of virtuous character,

more valuable than jewels . . . her children rise up

and call her blessed; her husband also."

CONTENTS

FOREWORD

HANK HANEGRAAFF has earned a reputation as a
superlative Bible teacher and as a vibrant radio presence to whom many thousands of listeners turn
when they need answers to hard questions. The
subject of evolution needs as much good teaching as
it can get. As one who has plowed that bit of field
myself, I'm delighted to see Hank bringing his very
special skills to the task of showing Christians what is
at stake in the evolution controversy and telling
them why they can't afford to ignore it.

Hank Hanegraaff doesn't advise parents and
teachers to hide from false teaching. He gives them
memorable teaching devices to help them identify
the fallacies and to help them teach young people
not to be misled. He exposes the specific wrong

answers and provides lots of references to other litera-
ture. Finally, he encourages us to stay with the big
picture and not to go off on matters of detail that
divide the faithful and give ammunition to the
agnostics.

Hank has done his many admirers a great service
by providing this very helpful book. I hope that those
who read it and learn from it will help us to create a
new generation of educated Christians who stand up
for good science, but who also know how to expose
the bad thinking and hidden philosophical assumptions so pervasive in evolutionary theory.

—PHILLIP E. JOHNSON
Jefferson E. Peyser Professor of Law Emeritus
University of California, Berkeley

ACKNOWLEDGMENTS

As with the world, this work did not come into being because of blind evolutionary processes. Rather, it was created through years of research and reflection. As the notes demonstrate, I am deeply indebted to the input and insight of hundreds of authors and resources. Futhermore, I am grateful for my family and the wonderfully cohesive board and staff that God has allowed us to assemble at the Christian Research Institute. Finally, I would like to acknowledge the staff of W Publishing Group for their support. Above all, I am grateful to my heavenly Father for giving me the commitment and creativity necessary to complete this task. To Him be the glory!

INTRODUCTION

On December 27, 1831, Charles Darwin left Devonport, England, aboard Her Majesty's ship, the *Beagle*. As Darwin set sail, he was a Bible-believing creationist. In his words, "I did not then in the least doubt the strict and literal truth of every word in the Bible. . . ."[1] However, as Dr. Michael Denton points out:

> For Darwin the *Beagle* proved the turning point of his life, a liberating journey through time and space which freed him from the constraining influence of Genesis. Every voyage conjures up a vision of new horizons and emancipation, but there is something particularly evocative about the voyage on the *Beagle* to the remote and little known shores of South

America. It is almost as if the elemental forces of
nature, so apparent along those cold and stormy coasts
of Patagonia and Tierra del Fuego, had conspired
together to fragment the whole framework of biblical
literalism in Darwin's mind, to blow his intellect clear
of all the accumulated cobwebs of tradition and
religious obscurantism. The *Beagle* is also symbolic
of the much greater voyage which the whole of our
culture subsequently made from the narrow funda-
mentalism of the Victorian era to the skepticism and
uncertainty of the twentieth century. Darwin's experi-
ences during those liberating five years became the
experience of the world.[2]

Denton goes on to demonstrate that what Darwin
saw as the liberating worldview of evolution has in
reality led civilization into a monstrous lie. Darwin's
journey on the *Beagle* sowed seeds of doubt in his
mind regarding creationism. As you continue
through the pages of this book, you will discover that
his doubts were totally unwarranted.

When Darwin charted his course, he did not
know where his journey would lead. In contrast, as

you travel through these pages, I want you to know
exactly where you are going and how you will get
there. If you begin as a creationist, you will become
equipped to demonstrate the fatal flaws of evolution.
In addition, your confidence in the Christian worldview will be solidified. If you begin as an evolutionist, the shaky pillars of your worldview will be
undermined.

TRUTH OR CONSEQUENCES

We begin our journey with a chapter titled "Truth or
Consequences." As you progress through this
section, you will discover that more consequences
for society hinge on the issue of human origins than
on any other. Among them are the *sovereignty of self,*
the *sexual revolution,* and *survival of the fittest.*

To make the heart of this material memorable, I
developed chapters 2 through 5 around the acronym
F-A-C-E. For generations, the "face" of *Pithecanthropus
erectus* has been used covertly to communicate the
notion that evolution is based in fact. I will now use it
overtly to demonstrate that evolution is a farce.

FOSSIL FOLLIES

The *F* in FACE will serve to remind us that the fossil record is an embarrassment to evolutionists. It demonstrates that transitional forms from one kind to another are purely mythological. While the general public seems blithely unaware of the fact that transitions from one kind to another do not exist, it is common knowledge among paleontologists. As we see in chapter 2, that is precisely why novel theories involving *pseudosaurs, pro-avises,* and *punctuated equilibrium* are constantly evolving.

APE-MEN FICTION, FRAUD, AND FANTASY

The *A* in FACE represents ape-men fiction, fraud, and fantasy. In chapter 3 you will discover that *Pithecanthropus erectus* is fictitious, *Piltdown man* was a fraud, and *Peking man* is pure fantasy. To say that "hominids" like Peking man and his partners are closely related to humans because both can walk is like saying that a hummingbird and a helicopter are closely related because both can fly. The distance between an ape who cannot read or write and a descendant of

Adam who can compose a musical masterpiece or send someone to the moon is the distance of infinity.

CHANCE

C stands for chance. Imagine asserting that the majestic *Messiah* composed itself apart from Handel or that the *Last Supper* painted itself without Leonardo da Vinci. In chapter 4 we will consider some even more egregious notions—that an *eye*, an *egg*, or the *earth*, each in its vast complexity, came into existence by blind chance. As we will see, forming even a protein molecule by random processes is not only improbable but is also, indeed, impossible.

EMPIRICAL SCIENCE

E represents empirical science. In chapter 5 we will test the theory of evolution in light of reason and empirical science rather than rhetoric and emotional stereotypes. As you will discover, the basic laws of science, including the laws of *effects* and their causes, *energy conservation*, and *entropy* undergird the creation model for origins and undermine the evolutionary model.

RECAPITULATION

Up to this point we have used FACE as an acronym to equip you to remember the arguments for responding to the farce of evolution. In chapter 6 we will insert the letter R and change F-A-C-E into F-A-R-C-E. Here, *R* equals recapitulation. This letter will remind you of the recapitulation theory, commonly referred to by the evolutionary cliché, "Ontogeny recapitulates phylogeny." This notion suggests that in the course of an embryo's development (ontogeny), it repeats (recapitulates) the evolutionary history of its species (phylogeny). Thus, at various points the emerging embryo is a fish, then a frog, and finally a fetus. This theory not only relies on *revisionist* history but has also been used as justification for *Roe v. Wade* and for *racism*.

TRUTH OR CONSEQUENCES

OTHER THAN SCRIPTURE, Darwin's magnum opus, *The Origin of Species by Means of Natural Selection*, might well be the most significant literary work in the annals of recorded history. Sir Julian Huxley called the evolutionary dogma it spawned "the most powerful and most comprehensive idea that has ever arisen on earth."[1]

Harvard scientist Ernst Mayr said that the Darwinian revolution of 1859 was "perhaps the most fundamental of all intellectual revolutions in the history of mankind."[2] Likewise, Dr. Michael Denton points out that the far-reaching effects of the Darwinian dogma ignited an intellectual revolution more significant than the Copernican and Newtonian revolutions. He goes on to say,

The triumph of evolution meant the end of the traditional belief in the world as a purposeful created order—the so-called teleological outlook which had been predominant in the western world for two millennia. According to Darwin, all the design, order and complexity of life and the eerie purposefulness of living systems were the result of a simple blind random process—natural selection. Before Darwin, men had believed a providential intelligence had imposed its mysterious design upon nature, but now chance ruled supreme. God's will was replaced by the capriciousness of a roulette wheel. The break with the past was complete.[3]

It would be impossible to overstate the significance of Darwinian evolution. As Denton underscores, the twentieth century cannot be comprehended apart from the intellectual revolution the theory produced:

The social and political currents which have swept the world in the past eighty years would have been impossible without its intellectual sanction. It is ironic to recall that it was the increasingly secular outlook in the nineteenth century which initially eased the way for the acceptance of evolution, while today it is perhaps the Darwinian view of nature more than any other that is responsible for the agnostic and sceptical outlook of the twentieth century. What was once a deduction from materialism has today become its foundation.[4]

In light of this unprecedented impact of Darwinian dogma, it would be reasonable to expect it to be solidly rooted in truth. In reality, as this book will demonstrate conclusively, evolution is rooted in metaphysical contentions and mythological tales. Denton aptly summed up this sentiment when he termed the Darwinian theory of evolution "the great cosmogenic myth of the twentieth century."[5]

The far-reaching consequences of this cosmogenic myth can be felt in "virtually every field—every discipline of study, every level of education, and every area of practice."[6] The most significant consequence, however, is that it undermines the very foundation of Christianity. If indeed evolution is reflective of the laws of science, then Genesis must be reflective of the flaws of Scripture. And if the foundation of Christianity is flawed, the superstructure is destined to fall. Noted atheist G. Richard Bozarth understood this full well when he penned the following words:

> Christianity is—must be!—totally committed to the special creation as described in Genesis, and Christianity must fight with its full might, fair or foul, against the theory of evolution. . . . It becomes clear now that the whole justification of Jesus' life and death is predicated on the existence of Adam and the forbidden fruit he and Eve ate. Without the original sin, who needs to be redeemed? Without Adam's fall into a life of constant sin terminated by death, what purpose is there to Christianity? None. . . . What this all means is that Christianity cannot lose the *Genesis* account of creation like it could lose the doctrine of geocentricism and get along. The battle must be waged, for Christianity is fighting for its very life.[7]

While Bozarth predicted the demise of Christianity without Genesis, he might just as well have predicted the demise of civilization without God. Friedrich Nietzsche, who provided the philosophical framework for Hitler's Germany, understood this better than most. Thus, he predicted that the death of God in the nineteenth century would ensure that the twentieth century would be the bloodiest century in human history.[8]

In the final analysis more consequences for society hinge on the issue of human origins than on any other. Among them are the *sovereignty of self*, the *sexual revolution*, and *survival of the fittest*.

SOVEREIGNTY OF SELF

The supposed death of God ushered in an era in which humans proclaimed themselves sovereigns of the universe. Nowhere was this more evident than at the Darwinian Centennial Convention, which celebrated the hundredth anniversary of the publication of Darwin's *The Origin of Species by Means of Natural Selection*. With pomp and ceremony Sir Julian Huxley, the great-grandson of Thomas Huxley,

Darwin's bulldog, boasted, "In the evolutionary system of thought there is no longer need or room for the supernatural. The earth was not created; it evolved. So did all the animals and plants that inhabit it, including our human selves, mind and soul, as well as brain and body. So did religion. Evolutionary man can no longer take refuge from his loneliness by creeping for shelter into the arms of a divinized father figure whom he himself has created."[9]

While the evolutionary system of thought was credited for expunging the need for God, in reality it is merely the repackaging of an age-old deception. In the very first book of the Bible, Satan tells Eve that if she eats the forbidden fruit, "Your eyes will be opened, and you will be like God, knowing good and evil" (Gen. 3:5). What Satan was communicating was that Eve could become the final court of arbitration—she could determine what was right and what was wrong.

Humanity's newfound autonomy sacrificed truth on the altar of subjectivism. Ethics and morals were no longer determined on the basis of objective standards but rather by the size and strength of the latest lobby group. With no enduring reference point, societal norms were reduced to a matter of preference.

One of the most devastating consequences of humanity's repackaging of Satan's age-old deception was the sexual revolution.

SEXUAL REVOLUTION

Years ago noted evolutionist Aldous Huxley and his peers argued that the theory of evolution supported the assumption that there was no meaning to the world and therefore life could be lived without moral restrictions. Huxley wrote, "Like so many of my contemporaries, I took it for granted that there was no meaning [to the world]. This was partly due to the fact that I shared the common belief that the scientific picture of an abstraction from reality was a true picture of reality as a whole; partly also to other, non-intellectual reasons. I had motives for not wanting the world to have a meaning; consequently assumed that it had none, and was able without any difficulty to find satisfying reasons for this assumption."

Huxley went on to say, "For myself, as, no doubt,

for most of my contemporaries, the philosophy of meaninglessness was essentially an instrument of liberation. The liberation we desired was simultaneously liberation from a certain political and economic system and liberation from a certain system of morality. We objected to the morality because it interfered with our sexual freedom."[10] As such, evolution provided the ultimate escape from God. What we got in return was adultery, abortion, and AIDS.

Adultery has become commonplace as people fixate on feelings instead of fidelity. It is not surprising that nearly half of all new marriages end in divorce.[11] Abortion has become epidemic as people embrace expediency over ethics. In America alone the death toll for preborn children has exceeded 43 million.[12] AIDS has become pandemic. As people clamor for condoms rather than for commitment, more people have died worldwide from AIDS than America has lost in all of its wars combined.[13]

Attempting to rationalize God out of existence in order to do away with His laws of morality is as absurd as voting to repeal the law of gravity because people have fallen off of buildings, bridges, or boats.

Even a unanimous vote could not change the deadly consequences for someone who later attempts to jump off of a ten-story building. We cannot violate God's physical or moral laws without suffering disillusionment, destruction, and even death.

SURVIVAL OF THE FITTEST

Evolutionism not only dispenses with God and attempts to make humans the center of the universe, but evolutionism is racist as well. Consider the following excerpt from a letter written by Charles Darwin in 1881: "The more civilized so-called *Caucasian races* have beaten the Turkish hollow in the struggle for existence. Looking to the world at no very distant date, what an endless number of the *lower races* will have been *eliminated* by the *higher civilized races* throughout the world."[14]

Lest this be considered merely an aberration, note that Darwin repeated this sentiment in his book *The Descent of Man*. He speculated, "At some future period, not very distant as measured by centuries, the civilized races of man will almost certainly exterminate, and replace, the savage races throughout the world."[15] In addition, he subtitled his magnum opus *The Preservation of Favored Races in the Struggle for Life.*[16]

And Darwin was not alone in his racist ideology. Thomas Huxley, who coined the term *agnostic*[17] and was the man most responsible for advancing Darwinian doctrine, argued that "no rational man, cognizant of the facts, believes that the average Negro is the *equal, still less the superior,* of the white man. . . . It is simply incredible [to think] that . . . he will be able to compete successfully with his *bigger-brained and smaller-jawed rival,* in a contest which is to be carried on by *thoughts* and not by *bites.*"[18]

Huxley was not only militantly racist but also lectured frequently against the resurrection of Jesus Christ, in whom "[we] are all one" (Gal. 3:28). In sharp distinction to the writings of such noted evolutionists as Hrdlicka, Haeckel, and Hooton,[19] biblical Christianity makes it crystal clear that in Christ "there is neither Jew nor Greek, slave nor free, male nor female" (Gal. 3:28).[20]

It is significant to note that some of the Crusaders and others who used force to further their creeds in the name of God were acting in direct opposition to the teachings of Christ. The teachings of Huxley and others like him, however, are completely consistent with the teachings of Darwin. Indeed, social Darwinism has provided the scientific substructure for some of the most significant atrocities in human history.

For evolution to succeed, it is as crucial that the unfit die as that the fittest survive. Marvin Lubenow graphically portrays the ghastly consequences of such beliefs in his book *Bones of Contention:* "If the unfit survived indefinitely, they would continue to 'infect' the fit with their less fit genes. The result is that the more fit genes would be diluted and compromised by the less fit genes, and evolution could not take place. The concept of evolution demands death. Death is thus as *natural* to evolution as it is *foreign* to biblical creation. The Bible teaches that death is a 'foreigner,' a condition superimposed upon humans and nature after creation."[21]

Adolf Hitler's philosophy that Jews were subhuman and that Aryans were supermen led to the extermination of six million Jews. In the words of Sir

Arthur Keith, a militant anti-Christian physical anthropologist, "The German Führer, as I have consistently maintained, is an evolutionist; he has consistently sought to make the practices of Germany conform to the theory of evolution."[22]

Karl Marx, the father of communism, saw in Darwinism the scientific and sociological support for an economic experiment that eclipsed even the carnage of Hitler's Germany. Marx's hatred of Christ and Christianity led to the mass murder of multiplied millions worldwide. Karl Marx so revered Darwin that his desire was to dedicate a portion of *Das Kapital* to him.[23]

Sigmund Freud, the founder of modern psychology, was also a faithful follower of Charles Darwin. His belief that man was merely a sophisticated animal led him to postulate that "mental disorders were the vestiges of behavior that had been appropriate in earlier stages of evolution."[24] Daniel Goleman points out that "the evolutionary idea that Freud relied on . . . is the maxim that 'ontogeny recapitulates phylogeny,' that is, that the development of the individual recapitulates the evolution of the entire species."[25] This notion, which I refute in chapter 6, supposes that the conceptus at one stage is a fish rather than a fetus (from the Latin for "infant") and is thus expendable. The human carnage that has resulted from this evolutionary dogma has eclipsed the atrocities of Hitler and Marx combined.

It should also be noted that Darwinian evolution is not only racist but sexist as well. Under the subheading "Difference in the Mental Powers of the Two Sexes," Darwin attempted to persuade followers that "the chief distinction in the intellectual powers of the two sexes is shewn by man's attaining to a higher eminence, in whatever he takes up, than can woman—whether requiring deep thought, reason, or imagination, or merely the use of the senses and hands. . . . We may also infer . . . [that] the average of mental power in man must be above that of woman."[26]

In sharp contrast to the evolutionary dogma, Scripture makes it clear that all humanity is created in the image of God (Gen. 1:27; Acts 17:29), that there is essential equality between the sexes (Gal. 3:28), and that slavery is as repugnant to God as murder and adultery (1 Tim. 1:10).[27] The consistent application of biblical principles inevitably leads to emancipation. The consistent application of evolutionary principles inevitably leads to enslavement. The tragic consequences of evolution can hardly be overstated. Denton correctly points out that it "is one of the most spectacular examples in history of how a highly speculative idea for which there is no really hard scientific evidence can come to fashion the thinking of a whole society and dominate the outlook of an age." Furthermore, says Denton,

Considering its historic significance and the social and moral transformation it caused in western thought, one might have hoped that Darwinian theory was capable of a complete, comprehensive and entirely plausible explanation for all biological phenomena from the origin of life on through all its diverse manifestations up to, and including, the intellect of man. That it is neither fully plausible, nor comprehensive, is deeply troubling. One might have expected that a theory of such cardinal importance, a theory that literally changed the world, would have been something more than metaphysics, something more than a myth.[28]

In light of the tragic consequences, it is incredible to think that evolution is still being touted today as truth. The responsibility of demonstrating that it is in reality a farce can no longer be left to a few hired guns in the bastions of higher learning. It is crucial that all thinking human beings become involved in the process as well. This is why I developed the acronym FACE — to make it easy for anyone to remember how to demonstrate the fatal flaws of evolution.

We begin with the letter *F*, representing fossil follies. Darwin had predicted that the fossil record would bear him out. In reality, the fossil record has become one of the greatest embarrassments to his legacy.

FOSSIL FOLLIES

COLIN PATTERSON, senior paleontologist at the prestigious British Museum of Natural History, which houses the world's largest fossil collection— 60 million specimens—confessed, "If I knew of any [evolutionary transitions], fossil or living, I would certainly have included them [in my book *Evolution*]."[1] His statement underscores the fact that the fossil record is an embarrassment to evolutionists. No verifiable transitions from one species[2] to another have as yet been found.[3]

Darwin had an excuse. In his day fossil finds were relatively scarce. Today, however, more than a century after his death, we have an abundance of fossils. Still, we have yet to find even one legitimate transition from one species or kind to another. David

16

Raup, curator of the Field Museum of Natural History in Chicago, underscores this fact: "We are now about 120 years after Darwin, and the knowledge of the fossil record has been greatly expanded. We now have a quarter of a million fossil species, but the situation hasn't changed much. . . . *We have even fewer examples of evolutionary transition than we had in Darwin's time.*"[4]

Ironically, while the general public seems blithely unaware that no transitions from one species to another exist (which would be necessary to prove macroevolution[5]), it is common knowledge among paleontologists. That is precisely why novel theories involving *pseudosaurs, pro-avises,* and *punctuated equilibrium* are constantly evolving.

PSEUDOSAURS (ARCHAEOPTERYX)

Whenever I say that there are no transitions from one species to another, someone inevitably brings up *Archaeopteryx.* This happens so frequently that I've coined a word for the experience: *pseudosaur. Pseudo* means false and *saur* refers to a dinosaur or reptile (literally lizard). Thus, a pseudosaur is a false link between reptiles (such as dinosaurs) and birds. The notion that birds evolved from dinosaurs has so permeated modern thinking that it is "commonly maintained that dinosaurs still survive today in the form of birds, their feathered offspring."[6]

Archaeopteryx—literally "ancient wing"—is said to have twenty-one specialized characteristics in common with particular kinds of dinosaurs.[7] However, as Dr. Duane Gish explains, careful examination has demonstrated that in every case these characteristics are genuinely birdlike rather than reptilian.[8] Myriad evidences demonstrate conclusively that Archaeopteryx is a full-fledged bird, not a missing link. Here are just a few.

First, fossils of both Archaeopteryx and the kinds of dinosaurs Archaeopteryx supposedly descended from have been found in a fine-grained German limestone formation said to be Late Jurassic (the Jurassic period is said to have begun 190 million years ago, lasting 54 million years).[9] Thus, Archaeopteryx is not a likely candidate as the missing link, since birds and their alleged ancestral dinosaurs thrived during the same period of time.[10] In addition, it should be noted that a great deal of controversy has occurred in the evolutionary community as a result of other bird fossils found in sediments classified by evolutionists as Late Triassic (*prior* to the Jurassic). According to this hypothesis, these birds would have lived approximately 75 million years earlier than Archaeopteryx and, in fact, at the same time as the first dinosaurs.[11]

Furthermore, initial Archaeopteryx fossil finds gave no evidence of a bony sternum, which led pale-ontologists to conclude that Archaeopteryx could not fly or was a poor flyer.[12] However, in April 1993, a seventh specimen was reported that included a bony sternum. Thus, there is no further doubt that Archaeopteryx was as suited for power flying as any modern bird.[13] As noted in the highly regarded journal *Science:* "Archaeopteryx probably cannot tell us much about the early origins of feathers and flight in true protobirds because Archaeopteryx was, in a modern sense, a bird."[14]

Finally, to say that Archaeopteryx is a missing link between reptiles and birds, one must believe that scales evolved into feathers for flight. Two basic theories have been set forth by evolutionists to bolster this notion.[15] The arboreal theory holds that wings and feathers developed in tree-dwelling reptiles that jumped from the treetops to escape enemies or to pursue food. Thus, they developed as a mechanism to help ease the animals' fall. The cursorial theory, on the other hand, views ancestral reptiles as ground dwellers that relied on speed for protection or to chase prey. The development of feathered wings and tails lessened wind resistance and supplied lift to increase their speed.

In either case, air friction acting on genetic mutation supposedly frayed the outer edges of reptilian scales. Thus, in the course of millions of years, scales became more and more like feathers until, one day, the perfect feather emerged. To say the least, this idea must stretch the credulity of even the most ardent evolutionists. Consider for a moment the meticulous engineering of feathers. Each is a masterpiece of detail and design.

The central shaft of a feather has a series of barbs projecting from each side at right angles. Rows of smaller barbules in turn protrude from both sides of the barbs. Tiny hooks, called barbicels, project downward from one side of the barbules and interlock with ridges on the opposite side of adjacent barbules. In some feathers there may be as many as a million barbules cooperating to bind the barbs into a complete feather, impervious to air penetration.[16] Furthermore, the positioning of the feathers is controlled by a complex network of tendons that allows them to open like the slats of a blind when the wing is raised. As a result, wind resistance is greatly reduced on the upstroke. On the downstroke, the feathers close, providing resistance for efficient flight. The fearsome flight of the falcon and the delicate, darting flight of the hummingbird clearly illustrate the profound aerodynamic properties of the feathered aerofoil.[17]

These and myriad other factors overwhelmingly exclude Archaeopteryx as a missing link between birds and reptiles. The sober fact is that Archaeopteryx appears abruptly in the fossil record, with masterfully engineered wings and feathers common in the birds observable today. As noted by evolutionist Pierre Lecomte du Nouy, an expert in the science of statistical probability, "We are not even authorized to consider the exceptional case of the Archaeopteryx as a true link. By link, we mean a necessary stage of transition between classes such as reptiles and birds, or between smaller groups. An animal displaying characters belonging to two different groups cannot be treated as a true link as long as the intermediary stages have not been found, and as long as the mechanisms of transition remain unknown."[18]

Likewise, Stephen Jay Gould of Harvard University and Niles Eldridge of the American Museum of Natural History, both militant anticreationists, conclude that Archaeopteryx cannot be viewed as a transitional form. Here's how they put it: "At the higher level of evolutionary transition between morphological designs, gradualism has always been in trouble, though it remains the 'official' position of most western evolutionists. Smooth intermediates between *bauplane* [basically different types of creatures] are almost impossible to construct, even in thought experiments; there is certainly no evidence for them in the fossil record (curious mosaics like Archaeopteryx do not count)."[19]

Pro-Avis

A few years after Harvard's Gould ruled out Archaeopteryx as a missing link, Yale's John Ostrom proposed a brand-new candidate called pro-avis. Unlike Archaeopteryx, no fossil evidence exists for pro-avis.[20] Since science could not produce, science fiction prevailed. Ostrom pictured a prototype in *American Scientist*, and pro-avis sprang into existence.[21]

The pro-avis fairy tale, like any good fairy tale, begins long, long ago with little pro-avises running around on two legs while they playfully caught insects in their scaly little hands. One fateful day an ugly little pro-avis we'll call Mike was born. Unlike his brothers and sisters, little Mikey had frayed scales on both of his hands. Because of little Mikey's imperfections, no one wanted to play with him. Sadly, he had to run around all by himself trying to catch insects. Suddenly, little Mikey discovered something miraculous. Insects stuck like magic to his frayed scales. The more he caught, the better he ate. The better he ate, the faster he ran. The faster he ran, the more his scales frayed. In time little Mikey's ugly scales were transformed into beautiful flying feathers. Soon little Mikey was able to catch insects that would normally have been beyond his reach. It wasn't long before all the little pro-avises wanted to be just like Mike. They began fraying their scales and in time, like Mike, their scales were transformed into fantastic flying feathers. And they lived happily ever after.

In fairy tales, frayed scales turn into feathers, and frogs turn into princes. In evolution all you have to do is add millions of years and little pro-avises turn into beautiful flying birds.[22]

Even the most doctrinaire evolutionists have come to the realization that fairy tales about pseudosaurs like Archaeopteryx and pro-avis simply won't fly in an age of scientific enlightenment. *Newsweek* summarized the sentiments of leading evolutionists gathered together at a conference in Chicago as follows: "Evidence from fossils now points overwhelmingly away from the classical Darwinism which most Americans learned in high school."[23] Rather than becoming creationists, however, evolutionists have simply become more creative.[24]

Punctuated Equilibrium

The newest fairy tale produced and proliferated in the evolutionary community is a theory called punctuated equilibrium. Its genesis appears to be found in the "hopeful monster" theory of a German geneticist named Richard Goldschmidt.[25] Realizing that there was no compelling evidence for evolution in the fossil record, Goldschmidt speculated that there must have been quantum leaps from one species to another. In his book *The Material Basis of Evolution*, he sums up his sentiments as follows: "The major evolutionary advances must have taken place in single large steps. . . . The many missing links in the paleontological record are sought for in vain because they have never existed: 'the first bird hatched from a reptilian egg.'"[26]

Since I am the father of nine children, Goldschmidt's hopeful monster theory should give me considerable concern. Each time my wife, Kathy, "infanticipates," I should hold down the hospital window lest when she gives birth, our new offspring tries to fly away. Obviously, this is not science; it's science fiction.[27] Tragically, however, this evolutionary fiction is being pawned off on impressionable children as though it were evolutionary fact.

In *The Wonderful Egg*, a book written for children, a mother dinosaur lays an egg that hatches into the very first bird. After growing up into a beautiful specimen replete with wings and feathers, it flies up into a tall tree and sings a happy song. The real tragedy is not that the little bird's song may well become a funeral dirge when it realizes it has no one with which to produce offspring. The real tragedy is that this book earned recommendation from the prestigious American Association for the Advancement of Science, the American Council on Education, and the Association for Childhood Education International.[28]

Even more tragic is the fact that Gould, one of America's most widely read evolutionists, came to the defense of Goldschmidt's nonsensical notion. In "The Return of Hopeful Monsters," Gould recounts the "official rebuke and derision" directed at Goldschmidt by the scientific establishment. He then predicts "that during the next decade Goldschmidt will be largely vindicated in the world of evolutionary biology."[29] Although his prediction has not come to pass, it has not stopped him from propagating a theory called punctuated equilibrium, which in reality is little more than a regurgitation of Goldschmidt's hopeful monster theory.[30]

According to Gould's theory of punctuated equilibrium, "a species does not arise gradually by the steady transformation of its ancestors; it appears all at once and 'fully formed.'"[31] As Gish explains, punctuated equilibrium proponents speculate:

> Once a species has developed, it proliferates into a large population and persists relatively unchanged for one, two, five, or ten million years, or even longer. Then for some unknown reason a relatively small number of the individuals of the population become isolated, and by some unknown mechanism rapidly evolve into a new species (by rapid is meant something on the order of tens of thousands of years). Once the new species has evolved, it then either becomes rapidly extinct or proliferates into a large population. This large population then persists

for one or more millions of years. The long period of
stasis is the portion of the process referred to as the
period of equilibrium, and the interval characterized
by rapid evolution is the punctuation—thus the
term, punctuated equilibrium.[32]

The problems with punctuated equilibrium
should be self-evident. First, this theory is motivated
by the lack of abundant transitional forms in the
fossil record expected by the standard evolutionary
model.[33] Thus, it is a classic argument from silence.
Furthermore, this convoluted concept flies in the
face of the science of genetics. As noted by Gish,
"The genetic apparatus of a lizard, for example, is
devoted 100% to producing another lizard. The idea
that this indescribably complex, finely tuned, highly
integrated, amazingly stable genetic apparatus
involving hundreds of thousands of interdependent
genes could be drastically altered and rapidly reinte-
grated in such a way that the new organism not only
survives but actually is an improvement over the
preceding form is contrary to what we know about
the apparatus and how it functions."[34]

Finally, the effects produced by "jumping genes" or chromosomal rearrangements would not produce a hopeful monster but a monstrosity. Even if, as postulated by punctuated equilibrium, the jumps do not go from reptiles to birds but from scales to feathers, the jumps are still too fantastic. Conversely, if the jumps are in reality rather insignificant, then we are right back at square one—gradualism.[35] And as noted by Gould, "The extreme rarity of transitional forms persists as the trade secret of paleontology."[36]

Creationists and Christians should be grateful for the candor of doctrinaire evolutionist Colin Patterson when he admitted:

> For over twenty years I thought I was working on evolution. . . . [But] there was not one thing I knew about it. . . . So for the last few weeks I've tried putting a simple question to various people and groups of people. Question is: "Can you tell me anything you know about evolution, any one thing, any one thing that is true?" I tried that question on the geology staff at the Field Museum of Natural History and the only

answer I got was silence. I tried it on the members of the Evolutionary Morphology Seminar in the University of Chicago, a very prestigious body of evolutionists, and all I got there was silence for a long time and eventually one person said, "Yes, I do know one thing—it ought not to be taught in high school."
. . . During the past few years . . . you have experienced a shift from evolution as knowledge to evolution as faith. . . . Evolution not only conveys no knowledge, but seems somehow to convey antiknowledge.[37]

Nowhere is this antiknowledge more readily apparent than in the fiction, fraud, and fantasy surrounding ape-men. In chapter 3 we will use the A in the acronym FACE to remind you that humans are made in the image of the Almighty, not the image of apes.

APE-MEN FICTION, FRAUD, AND FANTASY

IN 1922, A TOOTH WAS DISCOVERED IN NEBRASKA. With a little imagination the tooth was connected to a mythological jawbone, the jawbone was connected to a skull, the skull was connected to a skeleton, and the skeleton was given a face, features, and fur. By the time the story hit a London newspaper, not only was there a picture of "Nebraska man" but there was also a picture of "Nebraska mom."[1] All of that from a single, solitary tooth. Imagine what might have happened if a skeleton had been discovered. Perhaps a yearbook would have been published!

Sometime after the initial discovery, an identical tooth was found by geologist Harold Cook. This time the tooth was attached to an actual skull, and the skull was attached to the skeleton of a wild pig. Thus,

Nebraska man, known by the "scientific" designation *Hesperopithecus haroldcookii*, has been unmasked as a myth rather than a man in the making.

Ironically, while scientists were attempting to make a monkey out of a pig, the pig made a monkey out of the scientists.[2] While one would think this blunder would preclude the possibility of similar fantasies, a parade of pretenders continues to persist.

PITHECANTHROPUS ERECTUS

Speculation about *Pithecanthropus erectus*, the ape-man that walked erect, is far and away the most famous "ape-man" fiction still being circulated as fact. While over time he has evolved into a new classification called *Homo erectus*, millions regard him as a friendly ancestor, not just a fossil, and simply refer to him by the nickname "Java man."

It is generally known that Java man was initially discovered by a Dutchman named Eugene Dubois on the Dutch East Indian island of Java in 1891. What is not so well known is that Java man consists of nothing more than a skullcap, a femur (thigh bone), three teeth, and a great deal of imagination. Even more disturbing is the fact that the femur was found fifty feet from the skullcap and a full year later. Most unsettling of all is that for almost thirty years, Dubois downplayed his discovery of two human skulls (the Wadjak skulls), which he found in close proximity to his original "finds."[3] This alone should have been sufficient to disqualify Java man as humankind's ancestor.

In truth, the most thorough fact-finding expedition ever conducted on Java man utterly demolished Dubois's claims. This trek, commonly referred to as the Selenka Expedition, included nineteen evolutionists bent on demonstrating that the evolutionary conjectures about Java man were true. However, their 342-page scientific report demonstrates beyond the peradventure of a doubt that Java man played no part in human evolution.[4]

Despite all the evidence, it is truly amazing that *Time* magazine printed "How Man Began,"[5] an article that shamelessly treated Java man as though it were a true evolutionary ancestor. Even more incredible is the fact that Donald Johanson, best known for his discovery of a famous fossil named Lucy (after the Beatles' tune, "Lucy in the Sky with Diamonds"), still regards Java man as a valid transitional form; and Harvard's Richard Lewontin thinks this information about Java man should be taught as one of five "facts of evolution."[6]

PILTDOWN MAN

While *Pithecanthropus erectus* (Java man) can best be placed in the category of fiction, Piltdown man *(Eoanthropus dawsoni)* may be factually described as a fraud. While the fraud may have been cleverly conceived, it was crudely carried out. The jaw of an ape was stained to make it appear as though it matched a human skull; the Piltdown fossils along with accompanying bones were not only stained but also reshaped.[7] As Marvin Lubenow explains, "The file marks on the orangutan teeth of the lower jaw were clearly visible. The molars were misaligned and filed at two different angles. The canine tooth had been filed at two different angles. The canine tooth had been filed down so far that the pulp cavity had been exposed and then plugged."[8]

Despite the fact that the Piltdown fossils were clearly "doctored," highly esteemed scientists in the field affirmed their veracity. William Fix notes in *The Bone Peddlers* that the two most eminent paleoanthropologists in England at the time, Sir Arthur Keith and A. S. Woodward, declared that Piltdown man "represents more closely than any human form yet discovered the common ancestor from which both the Neanderthal and modern types have been derived."[9]

It wasn't until 1953, after the Nature Conservancy had spent a considerable amount of taxpayer money to designate the Piltdown site as a national monument, that Dawson's Dawn man (Piltdown) was formally declared a fake.[10] Although there is still a great deal of uncertainty as to who perpetrated the fraud, A. S. Woodward (keeper of geology at the British Museum), Pierre Teilhard de Chardin (a Jesuit priest), and Charles Dawson (the lawyer who unearthed Piltdown man in 1912) are front-runners in the long list of possible suspects.[11]

While Piltdown man may well be ranked as one of the most notorious scientific frauds in history, it was used for forty years to dupe unsuspecting students into thinking that evolution was a fact.

PEKING MAN

While Java man is fictitious and Piltdown man is a fraud, Peking man might best be described as pure fantasy.[12] Like Nebraska man, Peking man was based originally on a dusty old tooth. It was conveniently discovered in China, just as Canadian physician Davidson Black was about to run out of funds for his evolutionary explorations in 1927.[13]

The Rockefeller Foundation rewarded this discovery with a generous grant, permitting Black to continue digging. Two years later, he discovered what he fervently believed was Peking man's braincase, and he estimated Peking man to be half a million years old. Unfortunately, Black's fame was fleeting, for at age forty-nine, he died of a heart attack.[14]

Black's death, however, did not end his dreams. By the time World War II broke out, the evolutionary community had "discovered" fourteen skulls and an interesting collection of tools and teeth. All fourteen skulls were "missing in action" by war's end, yet the pretense persisted.[15]

The photographs and plaster casts that remained had some interesting similarities. Apart from the fact that the lower skeletons were missing, the skulls had all been bashed at the base. As Ian Taylor points out, Teilhard de Chardin of Piltdown fame made his former professor, Marcellin Boule, angry "at having traveled halfway around the world to see a battered monkey skull. He pointed out that all the evidence indicated that true man was in charge of some sort of 'industry' and that the skulls found were merely those of monkeys."[16]

Boule was not far from the truth. As Gish has pointed out in debates against evolutionists, it now seems likely that the tools found with Peking man were used on him, not by him.[17] It is now clear to anyone who looks at the evidence with an open mind that Peking man was not a distant relative but rather dinner.

To say that "hominids" like Peking man and his partners are closely related to humans because both can walk is like saying that a hummingbird and a helicopter are closely related because both can fly. In reality, the distance between an ape who cannot read or write and a descendant of Adam who can compose a musical masterpiece or send a person to the moon is the distance of infinity.[18]

All the evidence in the world, however, is not sufficient to convince those who do not want to be confused with facts.[19] To wit, Walter Cronkite, in the television premiere of *Ape Man: The Story of Human Evolution*, declared that monkeys were his "new-found cousins." Cronkite went on to say, "If you go back far enough, we and the chimps share a common ancestor. My father's father's father's father, going back maybe a half million generations—about five million years—was an ape."[20]

In fairness it should be pointed out that not all evolutionists believe humans evolved from monkeys. Some, in fact, believe quite the opposite—*that monkeys evolved from humans.* Geoffrey Bourne, former director of the Yerkes Primate Research Center of Emory University in Atlanta, Georgia, is a classic case in point. An article in *Modern People* points out that Bourne, who "is considered one of the world's leading experts on primates," believes that "monkeys, apes, and all other lower primate species are really the offspring of man."[21]

Bourne's beliefs are bolstered by an article in *New Scientist* in which John Gribbin and Jeremy Cherfas say they "think that the chimp is descended from man." Their theory is that "the genetic changes that produced early man from an ape were cleanly reversed to produce early chimps and gorillas from man."[22] The truth, however, is that evolutionists who believe humans evolved from chimps over millions of years, as well as those who believe chimps evolved from humans, are dead wrong.

No matter how many years the evolutionist postulates, chance operating on natural processes can no more create a chimp than it could create a cell. With that in mind, let's proceed to the letter C in the acronym FACE, which demonstrates that chance renders evolution not only improbable but indeed impossible.

CHANCE

ONE OF THE PRIMARY DILEMMAS of evolutionary theory is that it forces scientists to conclude that the cosmos in all of its complexity was created by chance. As biologist Jacques Monod, a winner of the prestigious Nobel prize, puts it, "Chance *alone* is at the source of every innovation, of all creation in the biosphere. Pure chance, absolutely free but blind, [is] at the very root of the stupendous edifice of evolution."[1] As noted theologian R. C. Sproul explains, for the materialist, chance is the "magic wand to make not only rabbits but entire universes appear out of nothing."[2] Sproul also warns that "if chance exists in any size, shape, or form, God cannot exist. The two are mutually exclusive. If chance existed, it would destroy God's sovereignty. If God is not sovereign, he is not God. If he is not God, he simply *is* not. If chance is, God is not. If God is, chance is not."[3]

Chance in this sense refers to that which happens without cause.[4] Thus, chance implies the absence of both a design and a designer. Reflect for a moment on the absurdity of such a notion. Imagine suggesting that Christopher Wren had nothing whatsoever to do with the design of St. Paul's Cathedral in London. Imagine asserting that the majestic *Messiah* composed itself apart from Handel. Or imagine that the *Last Supper* painted itself without Leonardo da Vinci.

Now consider an even more egregious assertion. Consider the absurdity of boldly asserting that an *eye*, an *egg*, or the *earth*, each in its vast complexity, is merely a function of random chance.[5] Ironically, Darwin himself found it hard to swallow the notion that the eye could be the product of blind evolutionary chance, conceding that the intricacies of the human eye gave him "cold shudders."[6]

EYE

In his landmark publication, *The Origin of Species by Means of Natural Selection*, Darwin avowed, "To suppose that the eye, with all its inimitable contrivances for adjusting the focus to different distances, for admitting different amounts of light, and for the correction of spherical and chromatic aberration, could have been formed by natural selection, seems, I freely confess, absurd in the highest degree possible."[7] He labeled this dilemma as the problem of "organs of extreme perfection and complication."[8]

Consider for a moment the incredible complexity of the human eye. It consists of a ball with a lens on one side and a light-sensitive retina made up of rods and cones inside the other. The lens itself has a sturdy protective covering called a cornea and sits over an iris designed to protect the eye from excessive light. The eye contains a fantastic watery substance that is replaced every four hours, while tear glands continuously flush the outside clean. In addition, an eyelid sweeps secretions over the cornea to keep it moist, and eyelashes protect it from dust.[9]

It is one thing to stretch credulity by suggesting that the complexities of the eye evolved by chance; it is quite another to surmise that the eye could have evolved in concert with myriad other coordinated functions. As a case in point, extraordinarily tuned muscles surround the eye for precision motility and shape the lens for the function of focus.[10]

Additionally, consider the fact that as you read this document, a vast number of impulses are traveling from your eyes through millions of nerve fibers that transmit information to a complex computing center in the brain called the visual cortex. Linking the visual information from the eyes to motor centers in the brain is crucial in coordinating a vast number of bodily functions that are axiomatic to the very process of daily living. Without the coordinated development of the eye and the brain in a synergistic fashion, the isolated developments themselves become meaningless and counterproductive.[11]

In *Darwin's Black Box*, biochemist Michael Behe points out that what happens when a photon of light hits a human eye was beyond nineteenth-century science. Thus, to Darwin vision was an unopened black box.[12] In the twentieth century, however, the black box of vision has been opened, and it is no longer enough to consider the anatomical structure of the eye. We now know that "each of the anatomical steps and structures that Darwin thought were so simple actually involves staggeringly complicated biochemical processes" that demand explanation.[13] Behe goes on to demonstrate that one cannot explain the origin of vision without first accounting for the origin of the enormously complex system of molecular mechanisms that make it work.[14]

EGG

In *Darwin's Black Box*, Behe further notes that there are black boxes within black boxes. As science advances, more and more of these black boxes are being opened, revealing an "unanticipated Lilliputian world" of enormous complexity that has pushed the theory of evolution beyond the breaking point.[15] Evolution cannot account for the astonishingly complex synchronization process needed for, say, the shell of an emerging egg to form from the calcium that is stored inside the bones of a bird's body.[16] This shell not only provides a protective covering for the egg but also provides a source of calcium for the emerging embryo and a membrane through which it can breathe.[17] Furthermore, evolution cannot account for the complex synchronization process needed to produce life from a single fertilized human egg.

"The tapestry of life begins with a single thread."[18] Through a process of incredible precision, a microscopic egg in one human being is fertilized by a sperm cell from another. This process not only marks the beginning of a new life but also marks the genetic future of that life.[19] A single fertilized egg (zygote), the size of a pinhead, contains chemical instructions that would fill more than five hundred thousand printed pages.[20] The genetic information contained in this "encyclopedia" determines the potential physical aspect of the developing human from height to hair color. In time, the fertilized egg divides into the 30 trillion cells that make up the human body, including 12 billion brain cells, which form more than 120 trillion connections.[21]

In Darwin's day, a human egg was thought to be quite simple—for all practical purposes, little more than a microscopic blob of gelatin. Today, we know that a fertilized egg is among the most organized, complex structures in the universe. In an age of scientific enlightenment, it is incredible to think that people are willing to maintain that something so organized and vastly complex arose by chance. As Dr. James Coppedge, an expert in the science of statistical probability, puts it, "Chance requires ten billion tries on the average in order to count to ten."[22]

In an experiment using ten similar coins, numbered one through ten, chance will succeed on the average only once in 10 billion attempts to get the number one followed in order by all the rest. Coppedge explains that if a person could draw and record one coin every five seconds day and night, it would still take more than fifteen hundred years for chance, on average, to succeed just once in counting to ten.[23] He goes on to demonstrate the difference intelligence makes by documenting that a *child* can do in minutes what *chance* would take a millennium to do. "Chance really 'doesn't have a chance' when compared with the intelligent purpose of even a child."[24] Even more revealing is the fact that a child playing the party game Scrabble can easily spell the phrase, "the theory of evolution," while chance requires 5 million times the assumed age of the earth to accomplish the same feat.[25]

EARTH

Like an egg or an eye, the earth is a masterpiece of precision and design that could not have come into existence by chance. Astronaut Guy Gardner, who has seen the earth from the perspective of the moon, points out that "the more we learn and see about our universe the more we come to realize that the most ideally suited place for life within the entire solar system is the planet we call home."[26] King David said it best: "The heavens declare the glory of God; the skies proclaim the work of his hands. Day after day they pour forth speech; night after night they display knowledge. There is no speech or language where their voice is not heard. Their voice goes out into all the earth, their words to the ends of the world" (Ps. 19:1–4).

Let's take a few minutes to explore the miracles that demonstrate life on earth was designed by a benevolent Creator rather than directed by blind chance.

First, consider plain old tap water. The solid state of most substances is denser than their liquid state, but the opposite is true for water, which explains why ice floats rather than sinks. If water were like virtually any other liquid, it would freeze from the bottom up rather than from the top down, killing aquatic life, destroying the oxygen supply, and making earth uninhabitable.[27]

Furthermore, ocean tides, which are caused by the gravitational pull of the moon, play a crucial role in our survival. If the moon were significantly larger, thereby having a stronger gravitational pull, devastating tidal waves would submerge large areas of land. If the moon were smaller, tidal motion would cease, and the oceans would stagnate and die.[28]

Finally, consider the ideal temperatures on planet Earth—not duplicated on any other known planet in the universe. If we were closer to the sun, we would fry. If we were farther away, we would freeze.[29]

From tap water to the tides and temperatures that

we so easily take for granted, the earth is an unparalleled planetary masterpiece. Like Handel's *Messiah* or da Vinci's *Last Supper*, it should never be carelessly pawned off as the result of blind evolutionary processes. Yet, tragically, in an age of scientific enlightenment many are doing just that. Consider the following introduction to *The Miracle of Life*, an Emmy award-winning PBS NOVA broadcast on evolution:

> Four and a half billion years ago, the young planet Earth was a mass of cosmic dust and particles. It was almost completely engulfed by the shallow primordial seas. Powerful winds gathered *random molecules* from the atmosphere. Some were deposited in the seas. Tides and currents swept the molecules together. And somewhere in this ancient ocean the miracle of life began. . . . *The first organized form of primitive life was a tiny protozoan [a one-celled animal].* Millions of protozoa populated the ancient seas. These early organisms were completely self-sufficient in their sea-water world. *They moved about their aquatic environment feeding on bacteria*

and other organisms. . . . From these one-celled
organisms evolved all life on earth.[30]

The real miracle of life is how someone could
stand for such nonsense in the twentieth century.
First, how could the protozoa be the first form of primitive life if there were already organisms such as
bacteria in existence? Molecular biology has demonstrated empirically that bacteria are incredibly
complex. In the words of Michael Denton,

> Although the tiniest bacterial cells are incredibly
> small, weighing less than 10–12gms, each is in effect
> a veritable micro-miniaturized factory containing
> thousands of exquisitely designed pieces of intricate
> molecular machinery, made up altogether of one
> hundred thousand million atoms, far more compli-
> cated than any machine built by man and absolutely
> without parallel in the non-living world.[31]

Furthermore, far from being primitive, the
protozoa that were thought to be simple in Darwin's
day have been shown by science to be enormously

complex. Molecular biology has demonstrated that there is no such thing as a "primitive" cell. To quote Denton again, "In terms of their basic biochemical design . . . no living system can be thought of as being primitive or ancestral with respect to any other system, nor is there the slightest empirical hint of an evolutionary sequence among all the incredibly diverse cells on earth."[32]

Finally, as Coppedge documents, giving evolutionists every possible concession, postulating a primordial sea with every single component necessary, and speeding up the rate of bonding a trillion times:

> The probability of a single protein molecule being arranged by chance is 1 in 10^{161}, using all atoms on earth and allowing all the time since the world began. . . . For a minimum set of the required 239 protein molecules for the smallest theoretical life, the probability is 1 in $10^{119,879}$. It would take $10^{119,841}$ years on the average to get a set of such proteins. That is $10^{119,831}$ times the assumed age of the earth and is a figure with 119, 831 zeroes.[33]

To provide a perspective on how enormous a one followed by 161 zeros is, Coppedge uses the illustration of an amoeba (a microscopic one-celled animal) moving the entire universe (including every person, the earth, the solar system, the Milky Way galaxy, millions of other galaxies, etc.) over the width of one universe, atom by atom. This amoeba is going to move the entire universe over one universe (the universe is 30 billion light-years in diameter—to calculate the number of miles multiply 30 billion by 5.9 trillion) at the slowest possible speed. The amoeba is going to move one angstrom unit (the width of a hydrogen atom, the smallest known atom) every 15 billion years (the supposed age of the universe). Obviously the amoeba would have to move zillions of times before the naked eye could detect that it had moved at all.

At this rate the amoeba travels 30 billion light-years and puts an atom down one universe over. It then travels back at the same rate of speed and takes another atom from your body and moves it one universe over. Once it has moved you over, it moves the next person and then the next until it has moved all 5 billion or so people on planet Earth. It then moves over all the houses and cars, the solar system, the Milky Way galaxy, and millions of other galaxies that exist in the known universe.

In the time that it took to do all that, we would not get remotely close to forming one protein molecule by random chance.[34] If, however, a protein molecule is eventually formed by chance, forming the second one would be infinitely more difficult. As you can see, the science of statistical probability demonstrates conclusively that forming a protein molecule by random processes is not only improbable; it is impossible. And forming a living cell is beyond illustration. As King David poignantly put it, "The fool says in his heart, 'There is no God'" (Ps. 14:1).

We now move to the letter *E* in the acronym FACE, which represents empirical science. As you proceed you will be equipped to demonstrate that the basic laws of science undermine the theory of evolution and undergird the fact of creation.

–5–
EMPIRICAL SCIENCE

Go to the classics section of virtually any video store and you will find *Inherit the Wind*, a propaganda piece starring Spencer Tracy and Gene Kelly. It features a fictionalized account of the 1925 Scopes trial, in which a teacher is jailed for violating a state law prohibiting the teaching of evolution. Creationists are portrayed as bigoted ignoramuses while evolutionists are pictured as benevolent intellectuals.[1] In the end, one is left with the notion that believing in the creation model for origins is tantamount to committing intellectual suicide. In reality, nothing could be further from the truth. Some of the greatest intellects the world has ever known were defenders of a creation view of origins.

Leonardo da Vinci, considered by some to be the

55

real founder of modern science, was a committed creationist. Robert Boyle, the father of modern chemistry as well as the greatest physical scientist of his generation, was a great apologist for the Genesis account of origins. Isaac Newton, a prodigious intellect who developed calculus, discovered the law of gravity, and designed the first reflecting telescope, not only refuted atheism but also strongly defended the biblical account of creation. Louis Pasteur, well known for the process of pasteurization and for utterly demolishing the concept of spontaneous generation, was devoutly religious and strongly opposed Darwinian evolution.[2]

Dr. Henry Morris devoted a book to "men of science and men of God," which includes other intellects including Johannes Kepler (scientific astronomy), Francis Bacon (scientific method), Blaise Pascal (mathematician), Carolus Linnaeus (biological taxonomy), Gregor Mendel (genetics), Michael Faraday (electromagnetics), and Joseph Lister (antiseptic surgery).[3] Albert Einstein, one of the greatest intellects of modern times, also "came to the conclusion that God did not create by chance, but rather that he worked according to planned, mathematical, teleonomic, and therefore — to him — rational guidelines."[4]

Rather than falling for rhetoric and emotional stereotypes — such as those presented in *Inherit the Wind* — these men were deeply committed to reason and empirical science. Like them, we would do well to test the theory of evolution in light of the laws of science instead of trying them in the court of public opinion.

EFFECTS AND THEIR CAUSES

In *2001: A Space Odyssey,* astronauts exploring the moon discovered an obelisk. Moviegoers immediately understood the import of the discovery. They may not have known whether the obelisk was designed by space aliens, angels, or the lost civilization of Atlantis, but they did know that an intelligent being had previously been to the moon. Had the plot of the movie attempted to suggest that the obelisk was an effect without an intelligent cause, it would have been laughed out of theaters.[5]

It doesn't take a rocket scientist to understand that an effect (an obelisk) must have a cause (a designer) greater than itself. As Fred Heeren points out, "This is common sense, and no one has ever observed an exception. Even Julie Andrews sings about it: 'Nothing comes from nothing; nothing ever could.' That every effect must have a cause is a self-evident truth, not only for those who have been trained in logic, but for thinking people everywhere."[6]

Cause and effect, "which is universally accepted and followed in every field of science, relates every phenomenon as an effect to a cause. No effect is ever quantitatively 'greater' nor qualitatively 'superior' to its cause. An effect can be lower than its cause but never higher."[7] In stark contrast, the theory of evolution attempts to make effects such as organized complexity, life, and personality greater than their causes—disorder, nonlife, and impersonal forces. As has been well said, "'Teleology is a lady without whom no biologist can exist; yet he is ashamed to be seen with her in public.' Design requires a designer, and this is precisely what is lacking in non-theistic [materialistic] evolution."[8]

In the television series *Cosmos*, Carl Sagan boldly pontificated—but never proved—his premise that "the cosmos is all that is or ever was or ever will be."[9] In stark contrast, Albert Einstein humbly acknowledged that "the harmony of natural law . . . reveals an intelligence of such superiority that, compared with it, all the systematic thinking and acting of human beings is an utterly insignificant reflection."[10] Long before Albert Einstein, another prodigious intellect, the apostle Paul, said essentially the same thing: "For since the creation of the world God's invisible qualities—his eternal power and divine nature—have been clearly seen, being understood from what has been made, so that men are without excuse" (Rom. 1:20). In commenting on this passage, Fred Heeren says,

This self-evident truth is the simple, rational deduction that all we see is an *effect* which demands a very great, supernatural Cause. The sun and the stars, the moon and this Earth could not have come from nothing. That's irrational—not just to the Western mind, but to the *human* mind. Every phenomenon in the universe can be explained in terms of something else that caused it. But when the phenomenon in question is the existence of the universe itself, there is nothing in the universe to explain it. No *natural* explanation.[11]

One more point needs to be made before we move on. In saying that the universe is an effect that requires a cause equal to or greater than itself, one may well presume that this principle would apply equally to God. This, however, is clearly not the case. Unlike the universe, which according to modern science had a beginning, God is eternal. Thus, as an eternal being, God can be demonstrated logically to be the uncaused first cause.[12]

ENERGY CONSERVATION

Today's physical sciences are built on three laws of thermodynamics that describe energy relationships of matter in the universe.[13] These laws were established as a scientific discipline by Lord William Kelvin (1824–1907), a committed Christian, who, like Einstein, was a brilliant intellect. *The New*

Encyclopedia Britannica states that he published hundreds of papers, was granted multiple patents, and that it was said of Lord Kelvin that he was "entitled to more letters after his name than any other man in Britain." One of his greatest contributions to science was his role in the development of the law of energy conservation.[14]

Like the law of cause and effect, the law of energy conservation is an empirical law of science. Also known as the first law of thermodynamics, the law of energy conservation states that while energy can be converted from one form to another, it can neither be created nor annihilated.[15] According to Isaac Asimov, it "is considered the most powerful and most fundamental generalization about the universe that scientists have ever been able to make."[16] Fred Heeren notes that the first law of thermodynamics means:

> Neither mass nor energy can appear from nothing. Such an occurrence would be "a free lunch," as big bang theorist Alan Guth likes to say, in contradiction to the common sense notion that there is no free

lunch. And yet, there is no denying that the universe is here; so the universe itself appears to be a free lunch. But from the laws of physics we see operating today, creation is impossible as an ongoing event. That is, the conditions that we know hold true in our present universe prevent any possibility of matter springing out of nothing today.[17]

From a purely logical point of view it should be self-evident that nothing comes from nothing. In other words, it is illogical to believe that *something* could come from *nothing*. Yet, this is precisely what philo-sophical naturalism—the worldview undergirding evolutionism—presupposes. This is analogous to the nineteenth-century concept of spontaneous genera-tion, the false belief that life forms could arise directly from non-living substances such as beer or sweaty clothes that were left undisturbed for several days.

In an age of scientific enlightenment we should know better than to believe in the evolutionary dogma that presupposes something comes from nothing. To hold to the law of energy conservation is to jettison impossible constructs for the infallible canon, which clearly communicates that since God finished the work of creating (Gen. 2:1–3), He has been sustaining (conserving) all things by His power (Heb. 1:3).

ENTROPY

While the law of energy conservation is a blow to the theory of evolution, the law of entropy is a bullet to its head. Not only is the universe dying of heat loss, but according to entropy—also known as the second law of thermodynamics—everything runs inexorably from order to disorder and from complexity to decay. The theory of biological evolution directly contradicts the law of entropy in that it describes a universe in which things run from chaos to complexity and order. In evolution, atoms allegedly self-produce amino acids, amino acids auto-organize amoebas, amoebas turn into apes, and apes evolve into astronauts.

Mathematician and physicist Sir Arthur Eddington demonstrated that exactly the opposite is true: The energy of the universe irreversibly flows from hot to cold bodies.[18] The sun burns up billions of tons of hydrogen each second, stars burn out, and species eventually become extinct. While I would fight for a person's right to have faith in science fiction, we must resist evolutionists who attempt to brainwash people into thinking that evolution is science.[19] Evolution requires constant violations of the second law of thermodynamics in order to be plausible. In the words of Eddington, "If your theory is found to be against the second law of thermodynamics I can give you no hope; there is nothing for it but to collapse in deepest humiliation."[20]

Rather than humbling themselves in light of the law of entropy, evolutionists dogmatically attempt to discredit or dismiss it. First, they contend that the law cannot be invoked because it merely deals with energy relationships of matter, while evolution deals with complex life forms arising from simpler ones. This, of course, is patently false. As a case in point, contemporary information theory deals with information entropy and militates against evolution on a genetic level.[21] While in an energy conversion system entropy dictates that energy will decay, in an informational system entropy dictates that information will become distorted.[22] As noted in *Scientific*

American, "It is certain that the conceptual connection between information and the second law of thermodynamics is now firmly established."[23]

Furthermore, it is boldly asserted that entropy does not prevent evolution on Earth since this planet is an open system that receives energy from the sun. This, of course, is nonsense. The sun's rays never produce an upswing in organized complexity without teleonomy (the ordering principle of life). In other words, energy from the sun does not produce an orderly structure of growth and development without information and an engine.[24] If the sun beats down on a dead plant, it does not produce growth but rather speeds up decay. If, on the other hand, the sun beats down on a living plant, it produces a temporary increase in complexity and growth. In the *Origins* film series, Dr. A. E. Wilder-Smith explains that the difference between a dead stick and a live orchid is that the orchid has teleonomy, which is information that makes the live orchid an energy-capturing and organization-increasing machine.[25]

Finally, it has been suggested by some evolutionists—who appear to suffer from a sort of cognitive dissonance—that the law of entropy might not have operated in the distant past. Creationist Dr. Henry Morris points out that "this assumption would be tantamount to the denial of the basic assumption of evolutionism, namely, that *present* processes suffice to account for the origin of things. In effect, this device would acknowledge the validity of the creationist approach, acknowledging that special creative processes operating only in the past are necessary to explain the world of the present."[26]

Thousands of years before empirical science formally codified the law of entropy, Scripture clearly communicated it. The prophet Isaiah and King David both declared that the heavens and the earth would "wear out like a garment" (Isa. 51:6; Ps. 102:25–26). Likewise, in the first century the apostle Paul looked forward to the day when "the creation itself will be liberated from its *bondage to decay*" (Rom. 8:21, emphasis added).

In summary it should be noted that philosophical naturalism—the worldview undergirding evolutionism—can provide only three explanations for the existence of the universe in which we live: (1) The universe is merely an illusion. This notion carries little weight in an age of scientific enlightenment. As has been well said, "Even the full-blown solipsist looks both ways before crossing the street." (2) The universe sprang from nothing. As previously demonstrated, this proposition flies in the face of both the laws of cause and effect and energy conservation. There simply are no free lunches. The conditions that hold true in this universe prevent any possibility of matter springing out of nothing. (3) The universe eternally existed. This hypothesis is devastated by the law of entropy, which predicts that a universe that has eternally existed would have died an "eternity ago" of heat loss.

There is, however, one other possibility. It is found in the first chapter of the first book of the Bible: "In the beginning God created the heavens and the earth." In an age of empirical science, nothing could be more certain, clear, or correct.

We have used FACE as an acronym to help you remember salient points to respond to the farce of evolution. You should now be equipped to demonstrate that

- the *F*ossil record is an embarrassment to evolutionists;

- *A*pe-men are fiction, fraud, and fantasy;

- *C*hance renders evolution not just improbable but also impossible; and

- *E*mpirical science supports the creation model for origins and militates against the theory of evolution. But there's more.

By adding the letter *R* we can change the acronym FACE into F-A-R-C-E. In this way you will be reminded of one more nail in the evolutionary coffin—namely, recapitulation.

RECAPITULATION

RECAPITULATION, better known by the once popular evolutionary phrase "Ontogeny recapitulates phylogeny," is the notion that in the course of an embryo's development (ontogeny), the embryo repeats (recapitulates) the evolutionary history of its species (phylogeny).[1] Thus, at various points, an emerging human is a fish, a frog, and finally a fetus. This theory, first championed by a German biologist named Ernst Haeckel, is not only based on *revisionism* but has also been used as justification for *Roe v. Wade* and for *racism*.

REVISIONISM

In *Ontogeny and Phylogeny*, Harvard professor Stephen Jay Gould points out that German scientist

Wilhelm His exposed such "shocking dishonesty" on the part of Ernst Haeckel that it rendered him unworthy "to be counted as a peer in the company of earnest researchers."[2] Tragically, despite acknowledging that the recapitulation theory has been discredited, Gould proceeded to write an entire book to demonstrate that it is still "one of the great themes of evolutionary biology."[3]

Sir Gavin de Beer of the British Natural History Museum was more circumspect. He was quoted as saying, "Seldom has an assertion like that of Haeckel's 'theory of recapitulation,' facile, tidy, and plausible, widely accepted without critical examination, done so much harm to science."[4] Haeckel not only utilized deceptive data but also used doctored drawings to delude his devotees.[5] His dishonesty was so blatant that he was charged with fraud by five professors and convicted by a university court at Jena.[6] His forgeries were subsequently made public with the 1911 publication of *Haeckel's Frauds and Forgeries.*[7]

Today the "recapitulations" most commonly referred to by educators and evolutionists are the "gill slits" in the "fish stage" of human embryonic growth.

Dr. Henry Morris notes several reasons that this supposed recapitulation is entirely superficial. First, the human embryo never at any time develops gill slits and therefore never goes through a "fish stage." Furthermore, a fetus does not have fins or any other fish structures. Finally, every stage in the development of an embryo plays a crucial role in embryonic growth. Thus, there are no redundant vestiges of former evolutionary phases.[8]

Although Haeckel's frauds and forgeries were exposed more than half a century ago, modern studies in molecular genetics have further demonstrated the utter absurdity of the recapitulation theory. The DNA for a fetus is not the DNA for a frog and the DNA for a frog is not the DNA for a fish. Rather the DNA of a fetus, frog, fish, or falcon, for that matter, is uniquely programmed for reproduction after its own kind.[9]

For more than a century it has been well known that what Haeckel referred to as "gill slits" are in reality essential parts of human anatomy. Far from being useless evolutionary vestiges, they are axiomatic to the development of a human embryo.[10]

ROE V. WADE

In *The Dragons of Eden* Carl Sagan stated that determining when a fetus becomes human "could play a major role in achieving an acceptable compromise in the abortion debate."[11] In his estimation the transition to human "would fall toward the end of the first trimester or near the beginning of the second trimester of pregnancy."[12]

Shortly before he died, I watched him reiterate this odd predilection. Using recapitulation as the pretext, he shamelessly defended the painful killing of innocent human beings. Without so much as blushing, he communicated his contention that a first-trimester abortion does not constitute the painful killing of a human fetus but merely the termination of a fish or frog. Thus in Sagan's world, *Roe v. Wade* provided the legal framework for the slaughter of multiplied millions of creatures rather than children.

Sagan was not alone in his rationalization for abortion. His appeal to the science fiction of recapitulation is common fare. Curtin Winsor, Jr., the ambassador to

Costa Rica, provides a classic case in point: In response to "After Roe," an article in the *National Review* by Father Richard John Neuhaus, Ambassador Winsor—with sarcasm dripping from his pen—wrote,

> If our well-meaning preacher has studied fetal anatomy, he might recall that the developing fetus actually retraces the evolutionary process. In a period of a few weeks, it begins as a single-cell creature and grows to be a fish (with gills), an amphibian, a reptile, and a mammal with a tail. Yes, at all times, this fetus has human potential, but that potential is implicit, not explicit, until around the twelfth week of pregnancy, when it manifests its human reality.[13]

Ambassador Winsor goes on to point out that recapitulation is a "reasonable basis upon which critical distinctions can be made in law." He specifically names "the law deriving from *Roe v. Wade*," which "gives the unwilling mother the benefit of the doubt, at least until her fetus is explicitly human."[14] A similar example of incomprehensible ignorance in an age of scientific enlightenment is found in the words of Elie Schneour, director of the Biosystems Research Institute in La Jolla, California, and chairman of the Southern California Skeptics Society:

> *Ontogeny recapitulates phylogeny.* This is a funda-
> mental tenet of modern biology that derives from
> evolutionary theory, and is thus anathema to
> creationism as well as to those opposed to freedom of
> choice. Ontogeny is the name for the process of
> development of a fertilized egg into a fully formed
> and mature living organism. Phylogeny, on the other
> hand, is the history of the evolution of a species, in
> this case the human being. During development, the
> fertilized egg progresses over thirty-eight weeks
> through what is, in fact, a rapid passage through
> evolutionary history: from a single primordial cell,
> the conceptus progresses through being something of
> a protozoan, a fish, a reptile, a bird, a primate and
> ultimately a human being. There is a difference of
> opinion among scientists about the time during a
> pregnancy when a human being can be said to
> emerge. But there is general agreement that this does
> not happen until after the end of the first trimester.[15]

Schneour, of course, is dead wrong; the notion that there is general agreement among scientists that a human being does not emerge during a pregnancy until after the end of the first trimester is merely the figment of a rather fertile imagination. While an emerging embryo may not have a fully developed personality, it does have full personhood from the moment of conception. French geneticist Jerome L. LeJeune bore eloquent testimony to this truth while testifying to a United States Senate subcommittee: "To accept the fact that after fertilization has taken place a new human has come into being is no longer a matter of taste or opinion. The human nature of the human being from conception to old age is not a metaphysical contention, it is plain experimental evidence."[16]

Dr. Hymie Gordon, professor of medical genetics and a physician at the prestigious Mayo Clinic, best summarized the perspective of science as follows: "I think we can now also say that the question of the beginning of life—when life begins—is no longer a question for theological or philosophical dispute. It is an established scientific fact. Theologians and

philosophers may go on to debate the meaning of life
or purpose of life, but it is an established fact that all
life, including human life, begins at the moment of
conception."[17]

RACISM

Roe v. Wade is not the only ghastly consequence of
the recapitulation theory; racism is another. This
point is amplified by none other than Stephen Jay
Gould, who notes that recapitulation served as a
basis for Dr. Down in labeling Down syndrome as
"'Mongoloid idiocy' because he thought it represented a 'throwback' to the 'Mongolian stage' in
human evolution."[18]

Tragically, as Gould points out, the term
"'Mongoloid' was first applied to mentally defective
people because it was then commonly believed that
the Mongoloid race had not yet evolved to the status
of the Caucasian race."[19] Dr. Henry Morris underscores the horror of this racist notion by noting that
recapitulationists not only believe that human
embryos recapitulate the evolutionary history of their

ancestors, but some like "Haeckel (and his disciple Adolph Hitler) used it to justify the myth of the Aryan superrace, destined to subjugate or obliterate other races."[20] In their view, a "Caucasian human infant had to develop through stages corresponding to the 'lower' human races (hence, the origin of the term 'mongolism') before becoming a full-fledged member of the 'master' race."[21]

It is incredible to think that in light of such evidence, evolutionists such as Winsor, an American ambassador; Sagan, a successful scientist; and Schneour, the chairman of a skeptics society, would champion recapitulation. It is equally amazing to realize that Henry Fairfield Osborn, the leading American paleontologist of the early twentieth century, had the temerity to say that "the Negroid stock is even more ancient than the Caucasian and Mongolian. . . . The standard of intelligence of the average adult Negro is similar to that of the eleven-year-old youth of the species *Homo sapiens*."[22]

Creationists can only be grateful that Gould has not followed suit. In an article titled "Dr. Down's Syndrome," he "decries recapitulation's responsibility for the racism of the post-Darwinian era."[23] In his words, "Recapitulation provided a convenient focus for the pervasive racism of white scientists; they looked to the activities of their own children for comparison with normal, adult behavior in lower races."[24]

Sadly, although Gould abandoned recapitulation, he never abandoned evolution. Instead, to the very time of his death he pitifully attempted to prop up the crumbling edifice of evolution with novel notions such as punctuated equilibrium.

THEISTIC EVOLUTION

It is one thing to believe in evolution; it is quite another to blame God for it. Yet under the banner of "theistic evolution" a growing number of Christians maintain that God used evolution as His method for creation. This, in my estimation, is the worst of all possibilities. Not only is theistic evolution a contradiction in terms — like the phrase "flaming snowflakes" — but as we have seen, it is also the cruelest, most inefficient system for creation imaginable. As Jacques Monod put it:

[Natural] selection is the blindest, and most cruel way of evolving new species. . . . The struggle for life and elimination of the weakest is a horrible process, against which our whole modern ethic revolts. . . . I am surprised that a Christian would defend the idea that this is the process which God more or less set up in order to have evolution.[25]

An omnipotent, omniscient God does not have to painfully plod through millions of mistakes, misfits, and mutations in order to have fellowship with humans. Rather He can create humans in a microsecond. If theistic evolution is true, Genesis is at best an allegory and at worst a farce. And if Genesis is an allegory or a farce, the rest of the Bible becomes irrelevant. If Adam did not eat the forbidden fruit and fall into a life of constant sin terminated by death, there is no need for redemption.[26]

Darwinism today is in much the same condition as Marxism was before its collapse. Its terminal condition cannot be successfully treated with medieval medications such as pseudosaurs or punctuated equilibrium. As the Soviet Union collapsed before our very eyes, so, too, the propped-up corpse of evolution is ready for its final fall. As mathematician Dr. David Berlinski eloquently satirized, "Darwin's theory of evolution is the last of the great nineteenth-century mystery religions. And as we speak it is now following Freudianism and Marxism into the Nether regions, and I'm quite sure that Freud, Marx and Darwin are commiserating one with the other in the dark dungeon where discarded gods gather."[27]

While insiders in the evolutionary community are aware of their theory's desperate condition, the general public is as yet in the dark. That's precisely where you and I come in. We have the inestimable privilege to share the news that nothing could be more compelling in an age of scientific enlightenment than: "In the beginning God created the heavens and the earth."[28]

NOTES

Introduction

1. F. Darwin, ed., *The Life and Letters of Charles Darwin*, vol. 1 (London: John Murray, 1888), 45, quoted in Michael Denton, *Evolution: A Theory in Crisis* (Bethesda, Md.: Adler & Adler, 1985), 25. The notion that Darwin was ever a Bible-believing creationist is widely disputed. In fact, his grandfather Erasmus—the real inventor of the theory of evolution—was an eighteenth-century rationalist.

2. Denton, *Evolution: A Theory in Crisis*, 25.

1. Truth or Consequences

1. Sir Julian Huxley, *Essays of a Humanist* (New York: Harper & Row, 1964), 125, quoted in John Ankerberg and John Weldon, *Darwin's Leap of Faith* (Eugene, Ore.: Harvest House, 1998), 39.

2. Ernst Mayr, "The Nature of the Darwinian Revolution," *Science* (2 June 1972): 981, quoted in Henry M. Morris, *The Long War Against God* (Grand Rapids, Mich.: Baker, 1989), 20.

3. Michael Denton, *Evolution: A Theory in Crisis* (Bethesda, Md.: Adler & Adler, 1985), 15.

4. Ibid., 358.

5. Ibid.

6.   Morris, *The Long War Against God*, 18.

7.   G. Richard Bozarth, "The Meaning of Evolution," *American Atheist* (February 1978): 19, 30.

8.   Cf. Morris, *The Long War Against God*, 72, 74. The tragic fact that the twentieth century witnessed more bloodshed than any other previous century nullifies an often-repeated accusation against Christianity, namely, that Christianity cannot be true because more suffering and death have resulted in the name of God than for any other reason. At the end of the twentieth century, however, with clear hindsight, we must not fail to recognize the ripened fruit of atheistic philosophies that have been fully actualized in this century's wars of extermination — in Marxist/Leninist totalitarianism, in Hitler's militaristic version, and so on (not including the horrendous holocaust of untold millions of babies through abortion). While it is tragically true that many people throughout history have misused the name of God to justify wickedness, there is no question that at the end of the twentieth century the blood of multiplied millions drips from the hands of the atheistic, materialistic mentality. (Thanks to Phillip Johnson for emphasizing this point.)

9.   Julian Huxley, Associated Press dispatch, Address at Darwin Centennial Convocation, Chicago University, 27 November 1959. See Sol Tax, ed., *Issues in Evolution* (Chicago: University of Chicago Press, 1960), 252, quoted in Henry M. Morris, *That Their Words May Be Used Against Them* (El Cajon, Calif.: Institute for Creation Research, 1997), 111.

10.   Aldous Huxley, *Ends and Means* (London: Chatto & Windus, 1938), 269–70, 273.

11.   See Rose M. Kreider and Jason M. Fields, "Number, Timing, and Duration of Marriages and Divorces: 1996," U.S. Census Bureau Current Population Reports, February 2002, 1, 18, http://www.census.gov/prod/2002pubs/p70-80.pdf, accessed 29 January 2003.

12.   The National Right to Life Committee estimates that the total number of abortions performed in the U.S. from 1973 to 2002 exceeds 43 million (see http://www.nrlc.org/abortion/facts/abortion-stats.html). The Alan Guttmacher Institute (AGI), a research organization founded by Planned Parenthood, reports that "nearly half of unintended pregnancies and more than one-fifth of all pregnancies in the United States end in abortion" (Lawrence B. Finer and Stanley K. Henshaw, "Abortion Incidence and Services in the United States in 2000," *Perspectives on Sexual and Reproductive Health*, [January/February 2003]: 6, http://www.agi-usa.org/pubs/journals/3500603.pdf, accessed 29 January 2003). AGI also reports, "Each year, more than half of unintended pregnancies worldwide—46 million, or two in 10 total pregnancies—are resolved by induced abortion" (Cynthia Dailard, "Abortion in Context: United States and Worldwide" *Issues in Brief* (1999 Series, No. 1): 2, http://www.agi-usa.org/pubs/ib_0599.pdf, accessed 29 January 2003).

13.   As of May 2001, the U.S. Department of Veterans Affairs accounts for 650,954 deaths in battle for all U.S. wars, plus 13,853 other deaths in service (in theater) and 229,661 other deaths in service (nontheater) (http://www.va.gov/pressrel/amwars01.htm, accessed 29 January 2003). The Joint United Nations Programme on HIV/AIDS estimates that in the year 2002 alone 3.1 million people

worldwide died from AIDS ("AIDS Epidemic Update" December 2002, http://www.unaids.org/worldaidsday/2002/press/update/epiupdate_en.pdf, accessed 29 January 2003).

14. Letter from Charles Darwin to W. Graham, 3 July 1881, *Life and Letters of Charles Darwin*, vol. 1, 316, quoted in Gertrude Himmelfarb, *Darwin and the Darwinian Revolution* (London: Chatto & Windus, 1959), 343, quoted in Henry M. Morris, *Scientific Creationism*, public school edition (San Diego: C.L.P. Publishers, 1981), 179; emphasis added.

15. The quote continues: "At the same time the anthropomorphous apes . . .will no doubt be exterminated. The break between man and his nearest allies will then be wider, for it will intervene between man in a more civilized state, as we may hope, even than the Caucasian, and some ape as low as a baboon, instead of as now between the Negro or Australian and the gorilla." (Charles Darwin, *The Descent of Man*, chap. VI "On the Affinities and Genealogy of Man," sect. "On the Birthplace and Antiquity of Man," in Robert Maynard Hutchins, ed., *Great Books of the Western World*, vol. 49, *Darwin* [Chicago: Encyclopedia Britannica, 1952], 336.)

16. It has been argued that Darwin, in the subtitle to *The Origin of Species by Means of Natural Selection*, probably does not intend, by the term *race*, to speak to the issue of distinctions among humans. However, his overall theory clearly does extend the meaning of *race* to encompass the concept of *subspecies* distinctions among groups of humans.

17. *Agnostic*, coined from Greek, literally means "someone who lacks knowledge." The term was suggested by Huxley in

1869 to refer to one who thinks it is impossible to know whether there is a God, or a future life, or anything beyond material phenomena *(Webster's New Twentieth Century Dictionary of the English Language,* unabridged, 2d ed. [New York: Simon and Schuster, 1983], 37).

18.   Thomas H. Huxley, *Lay Sermons, Addresses and Reviews* (New York: Appleton, 1871), 20, quoted in Morris, *The Long War Against God,* 60; emphasis added.

19.   Ales Hrdlicka (American Museum of Natural History) and E. A. Hooten (Harvard) were two of the founders of institutional physical anthropology in the United States. Ernst Haeckel developed the now debunked recapitulation theory (see chapter 6). These and many other influential men were not uneducated bigots, but they apparently really believed racism followed from their evolutionary science. See Morris, *The Long War Against God,* 60–68.

20.   It is a pervasive and consistent theme throughout Scripture that all people are created in the image of God and are of equal value (Gen. 1:27–28; 9:6; James 3:9; cf. Eph. 4:24; Col. 3:10). "From one man [Adam] he made every nation of men, that they should inhabit the whole earth; and he determined the times set for them and the exact places where they should live" (Acts 17:26). Also, to parallel Galatians 3:28, Malachi 2:10 reads, "Have we not all one Father? Did not one God create us? Why do we profane the covenant of our fathers by breaking faith with one another?"

21.   Marvin L. Lubenow, *Bones of Contention: A Creationist Assessment of the Human Fossils* (Grand Rapids, Mich.: Baker, 1992), 47.

22. Arthur Keith, *Evolution and Ethics* (New York: Putnam, 1947), 230, quoted in Morris, *The Long War Against God*, 76.

23. Jacques Barzun, *Darwin, Marx, Wagner* (Garden City, N.Y.: Doubleday, 1958), 8, cited in Morris, *The Long War Against God*, 83.

24. Daniel Goleman, "Lost Paper Shows Freud's Effort to Link Analysis and Evolution," *New York Times*, 10 February 1987, 19, quoted in Morris, *The Long War Against God*, 33.

25. Ibid.

26. Darwin, *The Descent of Man*, 566.

27. While Scripture candidly acknowledges the existence of slavery, it never condones it. In the last book of the Bible, Revelation 17–18, God pronounces final judgment on an evil world system that perpetuates slavery.

28. Denton, *Evolution: A Theory in Crisis*, 358.

2. Fossil Follies

1. Colin Patterson, personal letter to Luther Sunderland, 10 April 1979, quoted in Luther D. Sunderland, *Darwin's Enigma*, 4th ed. (Santee, Calif.: Master Books, 1988), 89. In a later interview, Sunderland asked Patterson whether he knew of any good transitional forms. Patterson affirmed his prior statement that he did not know of any that he would try to support. Sunderland writes, "Throughout his interview he denied having transitional fossil candidates for each specific gap between the major different groups. He said that there are kinds of change in forms taken in isolation but there are none of these sequences that people like to build up" (p. 90).

Patterson, of course, is a committed evolutionist. By "transitional form" I take him to mean a fossil that he can confidently say represents a form that lies between two fundamentally different species exhibiting wholly different structures and functions in an actual evolutionary line of descent—or that is directly ancestral to any such fundamentally different species. Furthermore, Patterson writes, "Fossils may tell us many things, but one thing they can never disclose is whether they were ancestors of anything else" (*Evolution* [London: British Museum of Natural History, 1978], 133, quoted in W. R. Bird, *The Origin of Species Revisited*, vol. 1 [New York: Philosophical Library, 1989], 183). Thus, while Patterson, along with most other evolutionists, does think that *Archaeopteryx*, for example, is evidence of some general evolutionary relationship between dinosaurs and birds (see Pseudosaurs, p. 17ff), he thinks he cannot say with any confidence that *Archaeopteryx* is an intermediate, transitional form in the actual evolutionary line between dinosaurs and birds.

2.   As Phillip Johnson has pointed out, the word *species* can be a bit of a trap. To evolutionists it can simply mean "isolated breeding groups," and in that sense trivial transitions can be said to have occurred. Of course, what we do not see are the sorts of transitions that would actually mean something and which evolutionary theory requires in order to stand: transitions between fundamentally different species that exhibit wholly different structures and functions (e.g., transitions between dinosaurs and birds, between apes and humans, etc.). (See also the distinction between microevolution and macroevolution in note 5, below.)

3.   The absence of verifiable transitions is striking in light of the fact that the theory of evolution utterly depends on the fossil record. Pierre-Paul Grasse, who held the prestigious Chair of Evolution at the Sorbonne for thirty years, wrote, "Naturalists must remember that the process of evolution is revealed only through fossil forms. A knowledge of paleontology is, therefore, a prerequisite; only paleontology can provide them with the evidence and reveal its course or mechanisms" (*Evolution of Living Organisms* [New York: Academic Press, 1977], 4, quoted in Henry M. Morris, *That Their Words May Be Used Against Them* [El Cajon, Calif.: Institute for Creation Research, 1997], 163).

4.   David M. Raup, "Conflicts Between Darwin and Paleontology," *Bulletin, Field Museum of Natural History* (January 1979): 22, 25, quoted in Paul S. Taylor, *The Illustrated Origins Answer Book*, 4th ed. (Mesa, Ariz.: Eden, 1993), 108; emphasis added.

5.   The theory of biological evolution maintains that living things (plants, animals, humans, etc.) have descended with modification from shared, common ancestors by unguided, purposeless, purely natural processes.

Macroevolution refers to large-scale changes—where kinds transform into fundamentally different kinds with new structures and functions. For example, birds are said to have evolved from dinosaurs; mammals eventually from fish; humans eventually from single-celled primordial life. This process would require the addition of new information to the genetic code.

Microevolution refers to changes in the gene expressions of a given type of organism but does not produce a completely different kind. For example, through selective breeding dogs ranging from Chihuahuas to Great Danes have been produced from wild dogs. This process, perhaps misnamed, does not require new information because the changes are a function of the genetic makeup already present in the gene pool of the kind. See also note 2, p. 87, note 33, p. 92, and note 25 pp. 99–101.

6.   Duane T. Gish, *Evolution: The Fossils Still Say No!* (El Cajon, Calif.: Institute for Creation Research, 1995), 130.

7.   Ibid., 133, citing A. J. Charig, *A New Look at Dinosaurs* (London: Heinemann, 1979), 139.

8.   Gish, *Evolution: The Fossils Still Say No!* 133 (see 133–39). Gish writes, "Since creatures within each family, order, or class are so highly variable, it would be predictable on the basis of the creation model that animals in different orders and classes would have some characteristics in common. Even humans share characteristics in common with reptiles. For example, we share in common the vertebrate eye. Among other characteristics, evolutionists emphasize that *Archaeopteryx* had teeth, a long tail, and claws on the wings, which, it is claimed, are reptilian characteristics, inherited from a reptilian ancestor. . . . [However,] *Archaeopteryx* did not have reptile-like teeth, but teeth that were uniquely bird-like, similar to teeth found in a number of other fossil birds . . . [having] unserrated teeth with constricted bases and expanded roots, while theropod dinosaurs, its alleged ancestors, had serrated teeth with straight roots. Furthermore, it should not be surprising that some birds had teeth, since this is true of all other vertebrates. Some fish have teeth, some do not. Some amphibians have teeth, some do not.

Some reptiles have teeth, some do not. Most mammals have teeth, but some do not. . . . The long tail is supposed to be a reptilian feature, but, of course, some reptiles have short tails, while many have long tails. . . . A number of modern birds have claws on their wings." (p. 138).

Sunderland notes that "the tail bone and feather arrangement on swans are very similar to those of *Archaeopteryx*" (*Darwin's Enigma*, 74).

9.   *The New Encyclopedia Britannica*, Micropaedia, 15th ed., vol. I (Chicago: Encyclopedia Britannica, 1981), 486. Gish, *Evolution: The Fossils Still Say No!* 133.

10.   Gish, *Evolution: The Fossils Still Say No!* 133.

11.   Ibid., 137, citing Tim Beardsley, *Nature* 322 (1986): 677; Richard Monastersky, *Science News* 140 (1991): 104–5; Alan Anderson, *Science* 253 (1991): 35.

12.   *The New Encyclopedia Britannica*, 486. Gish, *Evolution: The Fossils Still Say No!* 132.

13.   Gish, *Evolution: The Fossils Still Say No!* 133.

14.   Allan Feduccia, *Science* 259 (1993): 790–93, quoted in Gish, *Evolution: The Fossils Still Say No!* 135.

15.   *The New Encyclopedia Britannica*, 486. Michael Denton, *Evolution: A Theory in Crisis* (Bethesda, Md.: Adler & Adler 1986), 204–7. Gish, *Evolution: The Fossils Still Say No!* 134–35.

16.   Feather anatomy description adapted from James F. Coppedge, *Evolution: Possible or Impossible?* (Northridge, Calif.: Probability Research in Molecular Biology, 1993), 215. Denton, *Evolution: A Theory in Crisis*, 202.

17.   Description adapted from Denton, *Evolution: A Theory in Crisis*, 203.

18.   Pierre Lecomte du Nouy, *Human Destiny* (New York: Longmaus, Green and Co., 1947), 72. See also Gish, *Evolution: The Fossils Still Say No!*, 140–41.

19.   Stephen Jay Gould and Niles Eldridge, *Paleobiology* 3 (1977): 147, quoted in Gish, *Evolution: The Fossils Still Say No!* 139.

20.   Henry M. Morris and Gary E. Parker, *What Is Creation Science?* rev. ed. (El Cajon, Calif.: Master Books, 1987), 138.

21.   *American Scientist* (January/February 1979), cited in Morris and Parker, *What Is Creation Science?* 138.

22.   Comparing evolution to fairy tales was popularized by Duane T. Gish; see Gish, *Evolution: The Fossils Still Say No!* 5.

23.   *Newsweek*, 3 November 1980, quoted in Morris and Parker, *What Is Creation Science?* 142.

24.   If evolutionists begin with the presupposition that a Creator had no role in the origin of life, then they will not be swayed in the least by the absence of evidence for evolution and the abundance of evidence for creation.

25.   See Gish, *Evolution: The Fossils Still Say No!* 339–56.

26.   Richard B. Goldschmidt, *The Material Basis of Evolution* (New Haven: Yale University Press, 1940), 395. As quoted in Gish, *Evolution: The Fossils Still Say No!* 344.

27.   I first heard a version of this joke from D. James Kennedy in 1980.

28.   Morris and Parker, 148. *The Wonderful Egg* was published in 1958 by Ipcar.

29.   Stephen Jay Gould, *Natural History*, vol. 86, no. 6 (1977): 22, quoted in Gish, *Evolution: The Fossils Still Say No!* 341.

30.   Gould (Harvard University), along with Niles Eldridge (American Museum of Natural History) and Stephen Stanley (Johns Hopkins University), has been the main proponent of punctuated equilibrium. As noted by Gish, "Gould, apparently embarrassed by his rather hasty and overenthusiastic support of the hopeful monster notion which he had voiced in his 1977 article, was attempting to extricate himself by denying that Goldschmidt really meant what he had said" (p. 346). Gish, however, documents that Goldschmidt surely did mean what he said (see Gish, *Evolution: The Fossils Still Say No!* 344–47).

31.   Gould, *Natural History*, vol. 86, no. 5 (1977). As quoted in Gish, *Evolution: The Fossils Still Say No!* 346-47.

32.   Gish, *Evolution: The Fossils Still Say No!* 354–55.

33.   Standard evolutionary thinking assumes *gradualism*, which refers to the hypothesis that macroevolution (see note 5, p. 88) proceeds through the slow and basically constant accumulation of many small changes in order to effect large changes. Gradualism predicts that the fossil record would provide abundant evidence of finely graded intermediary life forms as one kind is progressively transformed into another.

34.   Ibid., 355.

35.   Morris and Parker, *What Is Creation Science?* 150. See also note 33, this page.

36.   Gould, *Natural History*, vol. 86, no. 5 (1977), 13, quoted in Gish, *Evolution: The Fossils Still Say No!* 346. More recently, Gould said that "paleontologists have discovered several superb examples of intermediary forms and sequences, more than enough to convince any fair-minded skeptic about

the reality of life's physical genealogy" ("Hooking Leviathan by Its Past," *Natural History* [May 1994]: 8). Remember, however, that it was largely the "extreme rarity of transitional forms" that Gould intended to explain with his theory of punctuated equilibrium. If hopeful monsters are not possible and gradual changes are not abundantly represented in the fossil record, the "several . . . intermediary forms and sequences" (none of which have been conclusively identified) are at best mysterious anomalies that will convince only those who look at the fossil record with a prior commitment to evolutionary theory. See also note 8, pp. 89–90.

37.   Colin Patterson, Address at the American Museum of Natural History, New York City, 5 November 1981, unpublished transcript. While Patterson's address raised much controversy, Phillip Johnson notes: "I discussed evolution with Patterson for several hours in London in 1988. He did not retract any of the specific skeptical statements he has made, but he did say that he continues to accept 'evolution' as the only conceivable explanation for certain features of the natural world" (Phillip E. Johnson, *Darwin on Trial*, 2nd. ed. [Downers Grove, Ill.: InterVarsity, 1993], 173).

3. Ape-Men Fiction, Fraud, and Fantasy

1.   *Illustrated London News*, 24 June 1922, cited in Duane T. Gish, *Evolution: The Fossils Still Say No!* (El Cajon, Calif.: Institute for Creation Research, 1995), 327–28.

2.   Adapted from Gish, *Evolution: The Fossils Still Say No!* 328.

3. Factual information adapted from Gish, *Evolution: The Fossils Still Say No!* 280–81. Marvin Lubenow explains that Dubois may well have concealed the discovery of the Wadjak skulls by declaring them only in "bureaucratic reports" that "were not intended for the public or for the scientific community" (Marvin L. Lubenow, *Bones of Contention: A Creationist Assessment of the Human Fossils* [Grand Rapids, Mich.: Baker, 1992], 104).

4. Lubenow, *Bones of Contention*, 115; see 113–19 for a good overview of the Selenka Expedition.

5. Michael D. Lemonick, "How Man Began," *Time*, 14 March 1994.

6. Henry M. Morris and Gary E. Parker, *What Is Creation Science?* rev. ed. (El Cajon, Calif.: Master Books, 1987), 154.

7. Lubenow, *Bones of Contention*, 40-43. William R. Fix, *The Bone Peddlers: Selling Evolution* (New York: Macmillan, 1984), 12–13.

8. Lubenow, *Bones of Contention*, 43.

9. Fix, *The Bone Peddlers*, 12.

10. Steve Jones, Robert Martin, and David Pilbeam, eds., *The Cambridge Encyclopedia of Human Evolution* (Cambridge: Cambridge University Press, 1992), 448.

11. Ibid. Lubenow, *Bones of Contention*, 42–43.

12. Peking man (originally classified as *Sinanthropus*) and Java man *(Pithecanthropus erectus)* have both been reclassified as belonging to the same species: *Homo erectus*.

13. Factual information adapted from Ian T. Taylor, *In the Minds of Men*, 3d ed. (Toronto: TFE Publishing, 1991), 235.

14.   Discussion adapted from Ibid., 236.

15.   Discussion adapted from Ibid., 237.

16.   Ibid., 240; some of the most interesting facts for reconstructing the Peking man story are found on pages 234–41.

17.   See Gish, *Evolution: The Fossils Still Say No!* 292–93 and Taylor, *In the Minds of Men,* 238–40.

18.   There are now thousands of hominid fossil specimens, ranging over a variety of classifications, including many other examples of fossils that were once thought to play a role in human evolution but have since been reclassified, such as *Ramapithecus* and *Homo neanderthalensis* (Neandertals). Even the Australopithecene hominids (of which the famous "Lucy" is an example) and *Homo habilis* are controversial among evolutionists. Though Christians disagree among themselves as to the dating of most of the fossils (and hence their classifications), it is even clearer now that there is not the smooth and finely graded transition from the earliest hominids to humans predicted by evolutionary theory. Rather, in accord with any biblical creation model, the data reveals recent and abrupt change with respect to both anatomy and culture between hominids and the appearance of humans (see Bloom, below). Just as all the major body plans of plants and animals appeared abruptly (and inexplicably for evolutionary theory) in the so-called Cambrian explosion, humans more so simply exploded onto the scene. For a "young-earth" perspective, see Lubenow, *Bones of Contention;* for an "old-earth" point of view, see John A. Bloom, "On Human Origins: A Survey," *Christian Scholar's Review,* Winter 1997, online at www.cccu.org.

19.   Evolutionary theory is so pervasive and has such a stranglehold on the scientific community that the pressure to conform all facts to the theory—no matter how contradictory to the theory the facts may be—is virtually insurmountable. In the field of paleoanthropology, in which evidence for evolution is particularly scant, the proclivity toward subjectivism is especially noticeable. This state of affairs largely explains the frequency of fantasy-filled fabrications in the history of hominid fossil studies. (See Phillip E. Johnson, *Darwin on Trial*, 2d ed. [Downers Grove, Ill.: InterVarsity, 1993], 81–87.)

20.   *Ape Man: The Story of Human Evolution*, hosted by Walter Cronkite, Arts and Entertainment network, 4 September 1994.

21.   *Modern People* 1 (18 April 1976): 11, quoted in Gish, *Evolution: The Fossils Still Say No!* 309.

22.   John Gribbon and Jeremy Cherfas, "Descent of Man—or Ascent of Ape?" *New Scientist*, vol. 91 (1981), 592, quoted in Gish, *Evolution: The Fossils Still Say No!* 311.

4. Chance

1.   Jacques Monod, *Chance and Necessity: An Essay on the Natural Philosophy of Modern Biology*, translated by Austryn Wainhouse (New York: Alfred A. Knopf, 1971), 112; emphasis in original. Monod eloquently explains the devastating consequences of his thesis: "The ancient covenant is in pieces; man knows at last that he is alone in the universe's unfeeling immensity, out of which he emerged only by chance. His destiny is nowhere spelled out, nor is his duty. The kingdom above or the

darkness below: it is for him to choose." (p. 180). Also quoted in John Ankerberg and John Weldon, *Darwin's Leap of Faith: Exposing the False Religion of Evolution* (Eugene, OR.: Harvest House, 1998), 21.

2. R. C. Sproul, *Not a Chance: The Myth of Chance in Modern Science and Cosmology* (Grand Rapids, Mich.: Baker, 1994), 9.

3. Ibid., 3.

4. Chance as an ontological entity does not exist. So when it is appealed to as an agency of cause, it is utterly impotent and meaningless. However, this sense of chance as a causal agency is what one gropes for in order to assert that universes appear out of nothing by chance. On the other hand, chance can quite usefully refer to formal mathematical probabilities, not at all signifying something that happens without a cause. In common parlance, when we say something has happened by chance, we don't mean that the event had no cause but that the actual cause is unknown to us. (See Sproul, *Not a Chance*.)

5. Perhaps we should generously give evolutionists the benefit of the doubt at this point and assume that reference to chance here is not as an ontological agency (referring to the notion of uncaused effects) but in the formal sense of mathematical probabilities, such that an already existent material universe through time and natural processes alone might manifest life through some discernible causal pathway. Of course, as we will see, life cannot be produced in this way either.

6. James F. Coppedge, *Evolution: Possible or Impossible?* (Northridge, Calif.: Probability Research In Molecular Biology, 1993), 218.

7. Charles Darwin, *The Origin of Species by Means of Natural Selection*, in Robert Maynard Hutchins, ed., *Great Books of the Western World*, vol. 49, *Darwin* (Chicago: Encyclopedia Britannica, 1952), 85.

8. Ibid. Of course, Darwin's lifework was intended to show that all biological organisms, with their attending "organs of extreme perfection and complication," were indeed formed through natural selection. See also note 25, pp. 99–101. Gordon Rattray Taylor points out further mind-boggling complications. Consider that in evolutionary mythology it is dogmatically asserted that snakes evolved from lizards despite the fact that the visual cells of lizards have no similarity to those of snakes. In addition, the eye appears suddenly in natural history, and even the earliest fishes have very sophisticated eyes. (Adapted from Gordon Rattray Taylor, *The Great Evolution Mystery* [New York: Harper & Row, 1983], 101–2.)

9. Eye description adapted from G. Taylor, *The Great Evolution Mystery*, 101–2.

10. See Ibid., 98–103.

11. See Coppedge, *Evolution: Possible or Impossible?* 218–20. Michael Denton, *Evolution: A Theory in Crisis* (Bethesda, Md.: Adler & Adler, 1986), 332–33.

12. Michael J. Behe, *Darwin's Black Box: The Biochemical Challenge to Evolution* (New York: The Free Press, 1996), 18. *Black box* is Behe's term for a device that does something but whose inner workings remain mysterious. For the average person, computers are a good example of a black box (p. 6).

13. Ibid., 22; see also 15–22.

14. In *Darwin's Black Box*, 18–21, Behe explains the biochemistry of vision, which serves as an example of a very complicated biochemical system that he hypothesizes is not gradually producible by successive minor modifications to some preexisting system because any slight modifications would not be functional, contrary to the predictions of evolutionary theory.

15. Behe, *Darwin's Black Box*, 8–10.

16. Coppedge, *Evolution: Possible or Impossible?* 216, citing T. G. Taylor, "How an Eggshell Is Made," *Scientific American* (19 March 1970): 89–94.

17. Christopher Perrins, *Birds: Their Life, Their Ways, Their World* (Pleasantville, N.Y.: Reader's Digest, 1979), 118–19.

18. *The Wonders of God's Creation: Human Life*, vol. 3, videotape (Chicago: Moody Institute of Science, 1993).

19. Ibid.

20. A. E. Wilder-Smith, *The Natural Sciences Know Nothing of Evolution* (Costa Mesa, Calif.: T.W.F.T. Publishers, 1981), 82.

21. A. E. Wilder-Smith, *The Origin of Life*, episode 3, videotape (Gilbert, Ariz.: Eden, 1983).

22. Coppedge, *Evolution: Possible or Impossible?* 50.

23. Ibid., 51.

24. Ibid., 53.

25. Ibid., 52. If chance is so inefficient at producing such a simple phrase as "the theory of evolution," it is just inconceivable to think that chance could have produced something as organized and complex as a single cell, let alone the unfathomable organized complexity of the human brain.

Evolutionists often acknowledge that accounting for the origin of first life by purely natural processes poses an intractable problem; but, they say, once primitive life appears on earth, this type of argumentation does not apply to the evolutionary paradigm. They suggest that rather than chance acting unilaterally on already living creatures to further evolutionary development, natural selection or some other unintelligent nonrandom mechanism takes over to produce "descent with modification" and the tremendous variety of organisms we find throughout natural history. Perhaps beneficial molecular genetic changes (chance *mutations*, where generally about one in 1,000 mutations are not harmful) are accumulated over time, while the actions of the environment on the plant or animal weed out harmful mutations (*natural selection*), thus accounting for the significant increase in genetic information necessary for large-scale evolution.

However, there is no solid evidence that information in the genetic code is or can be significantly increased through mutation and natural selection or through any other known natural mechanism. There simply are no known physical laws, or any known natural mechanisms involving any combination of chance and physical law, that can be invoked to account for the extremely high information content of genetic material. (See also note 21, pp. 106–107). Furthermore, it is a logical fallacy to say that an accumulation of beneficial changes will produce an improved overall design. Finally, those capable of scaling the evolutionary language barrier realize that this is little more than using the phrase "natural selection" while pouring the meaning of intelligent design into the words. (See Nancy R. Pearcey,

"DNA: The Message in the Message," *First Things* [June/July 1996]: 13–14; and David Berlinski, "The Deniable Darwin," *Commentary* [June 1996]. For an excellent discussion on the limited power of natural selection to effect evolution, see Percival Davis and Dean H. Kenyon, *Of Pandas and People: The Central Question of Biological Origins*, 2d ed. [Dallas: Haughton, 1993]).

26.   *The Wonders of God's Creation: Planet Earth*, vol. 1, videotape (Chicago: Moody Institute of Science, 1993).

27.   Adapted from Ibid.

28.   Adapted from Ibid.

29.   Ibid. Scott M. Huse, *The Collapse of Evolution*, 2d ed. (Grand Rapids, Mich.: Baker, 1993), 71. Huse lists a number of additional demonstrations of design, including: (1) "Any appreciable change in the rate of rotation of the earth would make life impossible. For example, if the earth were to rotate at 1/10th its present rate, all plant life would either be burnt to a crisp during the day or frozen at night." (2) "The earth's axis is tilted 23.5 degrees from the perpendicular to the plane of its orbit. This tilting, combined with the earth's revolution around the sun, causes our seasons, which are absolutely essential for the raising of food supplies." (3) "The earth's atmosphere (ozone layer) serves as a protective shield from lethal solar ultraviolet radiation, which would otherwise destroy all life." (4) "The two primary constituents of the earth's atmosphere are nitrogen (78 percent) and oxygen (20 percent). This delicate and critical ratio is essential to all life forms." (5) "The earth's magnetic field provides important protection from harmful cosmic radiation" (pp. 71–72).

30.   *NOVA: The Miracle of Life,* photographed by Lennart Nilsson, videotape (Boston: WGBH Educational Foundation, 1986, [Swedish Television Corp., 1982]); emphasis added. For a brief discussion, see Johnson, *Defeating Darwinism by Opening Minds,* (Downers Grove, Ill.: InterVarsity, 1997), 24–36, 123.

31.   Denton, *Evolution: A Theory in Crisis,* 250.

32.   Ibid.

33.   Coppedge, *Evolution: Possible or Impossible?* 110, 114.

34.   Discussion adapted from Ibid., 119–24.

5. Empirical Science

1.   For an excellent analysis of *Inherit the Wind,* see Phillip E. Johnson, *Defeating Darwinism by Opening Minds* (Downers Grove, Ill.: InterVarsity, 1997), 24–36.

2.   Discussion adapted from Henry M. Morris, *Men of Science, Men of God: Great Scientists Who Believed the Bible* (El Cajon, Calif.: Master Books, 1990).

3.   Adapted from Ibid. cf. Fred Heeren, *Show Me God,* rev. ed., (Wheeling, Ill.: Day Star, 1997), 334–63.

4.   A. E. Wilder-Smith, *He Who Thinks Has to Believe* (Costa Mesa, Calif.: T.W.F.T. Publishers, 1981), 70. Wilder-Smith writes, "It is, of course, clear that Einstein did not claim to be a Christian. His convictions in metaphysical matters reached only to a firm belief in a Creator, which motivated Einstein's research in mathematics and physics" (p. 71).

5.   Discussion adapted from Michael J. Behe, *Darwin's Black Box: The Biochemical Challenge to Evolution* (New York: The Free Press, 1996), 197.

6. Heeren, *Show Me God*, 88.

7. Henry M. Morris, *Scientific Creationism*, public school edition (San Diego: C.L.P. Publishers, 1981), 19–20.

8. Kenneth Boa and Larry Moody, *I'm Glad You Asked* (Wheaton, Ill.: Victor, 1982), 38–39.

9. Carl Sagan, *Cosmos* (New York: Random House, 1980), 4. The PBS television series *Cosmos* was closely scripted after his book.

10. Albert Einstein, *Ideas and Opinions—The World as I See It* (New York: Bonanza Books, 1974), 40. As quoted in Heeren, *Show Me God*, 92.

11. Heeren, *Show Me God*, 88–89. Besides an overwhelming preponderance of empirical evidence indicating that something does not come from nothing, which is foundational to the scientific enterprise of seeking causal explanations, simple logic requires that nothing cannot produce anything—for "nothing" does not *exist* and therefore has no *power to do* anything. The "power to do" logically presupposes the existence of the thing possessing that power. The only alternative would be that the thing said to be produced by nothing would have had to create itself. But if it created itself, it would have had to exist prior to its existence in order to do the creating, which means it must both exist and not exist in the same way and in the same respect, which is a violation of the logical law of noncontradiction (which says simply that a thing is not what it is not). If the laws of logic can be violated, then reason and communication are meaningless. Now, it is possible for something to exist without being the effect of a prior cause, but in order for something to exist and not

be an effect it must be eternal (i.e., something that did not come into being, but always existed). God is such a being. (See Norman L. Geisler, *Baker Encyclopedia of Christian Apologetics* [Grand Rapids, Mich.: Baker, 1999], 399–401; and R. C. Sproul, *Not a Chance: The Myth of Chance in Modern Science and Cosmology* [Grand Rapids, Mich.: Baker, 1994]).

12.   The argument for God as an uncaused cause goes as follows: While modern science affirms the fact that the universe had a beginning, and thus is not eternal, the materialist is left with a dilemma. Either the universe sprang from nothing by chance, or something unbounded by time and greater than the universe caused it to come into being. In other words, either something came from nothing or something is eternal. Since we have previously demonstrated the absurdity of suggesting that something comes from nothing (see also note 11, p. 103), we are forced to conclude that the universe was caused by something greater than itself—something or someone who ultimately is not dependent upon anything else in order to exist, something or someone who possesses the power of being, intrinsically, and therefore is eternal. This eternal being we call God.

Some might say that if the universe needs a cause, then the cause of the universe, too, needs a cause. This sort of reasoning is what led thinkers such as Bertrand Russell to wonder who or what created God. But we can easily see where this reasoning leads. We would have an infinite regression of finite causes to account for the universe, which is again akin to the absurdity of saying existence comes from nonexistence, since any series consisting of only caused causes cannot account for itself (it cannot answer the question of *source*, it merely makes the *effects* more numerous). Or we can practice good science and encounter an uncaused cause. Russell's counter that if God doesn't need a cause then neither does the universe completely ignores that the nature of the universe is finite, changing, and therefore not eternal—so it is reasonable to ask, "Who made the universe?" God, however, doesn't need a cause because He is infinite, unchanging, and eternal. The universe must depend upon something that can account for its own existence, something eternal and, therefore, uncaused. (See Geisler, *Baker Encyclopedia of Christian Apologetics*, 120–123).

13.   The first law of thermodynamics (conservation of energy) says that total energy, in all its forms, can neither be created nor destroyed, only shifted from one type to another. The second law of thermodynamics (law of entropy), in one of its several equivalent formulations, says that the amount of disorder in any isolated system cannot decrease with time. While the total energy in the cosmos remains constant, the amount of energy available to do useful work is always getting smaller. (Discussion adapted from Robert M. Hazen and James Trefil, *Science Matters* [New York: Anchor, 1992], 24, 29–33.) The third law of thermodynamics says that the entropy of any pure crystal at absolute zero temperature is equal to zero—in a perfect crystal at absolute zero there is perfect order. (James E. Brady and Gerald E. Humiston, *General Chemistry: Principles and Structure*, 2d ed. [New York: Wyley, 1978], 315.)

14.   *The New Encyclopedia Britannica*, Macropaedia, 15th ed., vol. 10 (Chicago: Encyclopedia Britannica, 1981), 415.

15. The energy equivalence of mass can be determined using Einstein's familiar formula, $E=mc^2$ (E is energy; m is mass; and c represents the speed of light).

16. Isaac Asimov, "In the Game of Energy and Thermodynamics You Can't Even Break Even," *Journal of Smithsonian Institute* (June 1970): 6, quoted in Heeren, *Show Me God*, 128–29; also in Morris, *Scientific Creationism*, 21.

17. Heeren, *Show Me God*, 128.

18. Ibid., 129.

19. If one advances all of the information on one side of an issue and suppresses information on the other side, that by definition is not education but an attempt to seduce or trick people into believing a particular story—some may call it an attempt at brainwashing. While brainwashing is not actually possible, much of what passes for science is nothing more than philosophical pontification. Naturalism, which says that nature is all that exists, has become what Phillip Johnson calls "the established religious philosophy of America," and anyone who attempts to buck this religious dogma faces tremendous pressure to conform. (For an excellent discussion, see Phillip E. Johnson, *Reason in the Balance* [Downers Grove, Ill.: InterVarsity, 1995].)

20. Arthur S. Eddington, *The Nature of the Physical World* (New York: Macmillan, 1930), 74, quoted in Scott M. Huse, *The Collapse of Evolution*, 2d. ed. (Grand Rapids, Mich.: Baker, 1993), 77–78.

21. The DNA molecule carries instructions for building unfathomably complex living organisms. Thus, information entropy is perfectly relevant to the discussion of evolution on a

genetic level. Information theory says that reduced entropy produced by random deviations is not equivalent to information — random processes do not produce information but rather distort information. Thus, random deviations in genetic material will not increase genetic information, which would be necessary for evolution to progress, let alone produce DNA in the first place. (See A. E. Wilder-Smith, *The Natural Sciences Know Nothing of Evolution* [Costa Mesa, Calif.: T.W.F.T. Publishers, 1981], 69–73.) See also note 25, pp. 99–101.

22.   Dr. Henry Morris demonstrates how the second law of thermodynamics (entropy) can be utilized in various contexts and defined in various ways, such as classical thermodynamics, statistical thermodynamics, and informational thermodynamics. In the first case, entropy is a measure of the unavailability of energy for further work. In the second case, entropy is a measure of the decreased order of a system's structure. And in the third case, it is a measure of lost or distorted information. In any case, what is being described is a downhill trend: Energy becomes unavailable, disorder increases, and information becomes garbled (adapted from Morris, *Scientific Creationism*, 38–40).

23.   Myron Tribus and Edward C. McIrvine, "Energy and Information," *Scientific American* 224 (September 1971): 188, quoted in Morris, *Scientific Creationism*, 39.

24.   Raw energy is no better than no energy at producing and sustaining life without something directing it—such as information and machinery. For example, a car sitting on an incline can progress downward by gravity but never upward without an engine that converts the raw energy of the gasoline in such a way

as to perform the work necessary to go uphill. Likewise, plants utilize the raw energy of the sun through the very complicated, information-dependent process of photosynthesis; without the information and machinery to perform photosynthesis, the sun's radiation would simply burn up the plant. As Morris concludes, raw energy without teleonomy is like a bull in a china shop, not a means of producing biological evolution. (For a helpful discussion see Morris, *Scientific Creationism*, 43–46.)

25.   Willem J. J. Glashouwer and Paul S. Taylor, *The Origin of the Universe*, videotape (Mesa, Ariz.: Eden, 1983).

26.   Morris, *Scientific Creationism*, 42.

6. Recapitulation

1.   William R. Fix, *The Bone Peddlers: Selling Evolution* (New York: Macmillan, 1984), 285.

2.   Stephen Jay Gould, *Ontogeny and Phylogeny* (Cambridge, Mass.: Belknap, 1977), n.430.

3.   Ibid., back cover. While admitting that the problems with Haeckel's recapitulation theory are myriad, Gould says he does not want to throw the baby out with the bathwater (see Ibid., 1–2).

4.   Gavin de Beer, "Darwin and Embryology," in S.A. Barnett, ed., *A Century of Darwin* (London: Heinemann, 1958), 159, quoted in Ian T. Taylor, *In the Minds of Men*, 3d ed. (Toronto: TFE Publishing, 1991), 274.

5.   Taylor, *In the Minds of Men*, 276. Taylor writes, "Haeckel stated that the ova and embryos of different vertebrate animals and man are, at certain periods of their development, all perfectly

alike, indicating their supposed common origin. Haeckel produced the well-known illustration showing embryos at several stages of development. In this he had to play fast and loose with the facts by altering several drawings in order to make them appear more alike and conform to the theory. . . . In a catalog of errors, His (1874) showed that Haeckel had used two drawings of embryos, one taken from Bischoff (1845) and the other from Ecker (1851–59), and he had added 3–5 mm to the head of Bischoff's dog embryo, taken 2 mm off the head of Ecker's human embryo, reduced the size of the eye 5 mm, and doubled the length of the posterior."

   6.   Walt Brown, *In the Beginning: Compelling Evidence for Creation and the Flood*, 6th ed. (Phoenix: Center for Scientific Creation, 1995), 45.

   7.   Assmusth and Hull, *Haeckel's Frauds and Forgeries* (India: Bombay Press, 1911), cited in Luther D. Sunderland, *Darwin's Enigma*, 4th ed. rev. (Santee, Calif.: Master Books, 1988), 120.

   8.   Adapted from Henry M. Morris, *Scientific Creationism*, public school edition (San Diego: C.L.P. Publishers, 1981), 77.

   9.   Adapted from Ibid. See pp. 75–78 for more detail concerning alleged evolutionary vestiges and recapitulations.

   10.   "The throat (or pharyngeal) grooves and pouches, falsely called gill slits, are not mistakes in human development. They develop into absolutely essential parts of human anatomy. The middle ear canals come from the second pouches, and the parathyroid and thymus glands come from the third and the fourth. Without a thymus, we would lose half our immune systems.

Without the parathyroids, we would be unable to regulate calcium balance and could not even survive. Another pouch, thought to be vestigial by evolutionists until just recently, becomes a gland that assists in calcium balance." (Henry M. Morris and Gary E. Parker, *What Is Creation Science?* rev. ed. [El Cajon, Calif.: Master Books, 1987], 64.)

11.   Carl Sagan, *The Dragons of Eden* (New York: Random House, 1977), 197.

12.   Ibid.

13.   Ambassador Curtin Winsor, Jr., "Letter to the Editor" in *National Review* (2 June 1989): 8.

14.   Ibid.

15.   Elie Schneour, "Life Doesn't Begin, It Continues," *Los Angeles Times* (29 January 1985): part v, quoted in Henry M. Morris, *The Long War Against God* (Grand Rapids, Mich.: Baker, 1989), 138.

16.   *The Human Life Bill: Hearings on S. 158 Before the Subcommittee on Separation of Powers of the Senate Judiciary Committee*, 97th Congress, 1st Session (1981), quoted in Norman L. Geisler, *Christian Ethics: Options and Issues* (Grand Rapids, Mich.: Baker, 1989), 149, quoted in Francis J. Beckwith, *Politically Correct Death: Answering the Arguments for Abortion Rights* (Grand Rapids, Mich.: Baker, 1993), 42.

17.   *The Human Life Bill—S. 158*, Report, 9, quoted in Beckwith, *Politically Correct Death*, 42.

18.   Morris and Parker, *What Is Creation Science?* 67. See Stephen Jay Gould, "Dr. Down's Syndrome," *Natural History* (April 1980): 142–48.

19. Henry M. Morris, *Creation and the Modern Christian* (El Cajon, Calif.: Master Books, 1985), 72.

20. Ibid.

21. Henry M. Morris, *Science and the Bible*, rev. ed. (Chicago: Moody, 1986), 50.

22. H. F. Osborn, "The Evolution of Human Races," *Natural History* (January/February 1926); reprinted in *Natural History* (April 1980): 129, quoted in Morris, *The Long War Against God*, 62.

23. Morris, *The Long War Against God*, 139.

24. Gould, "Dr. Down's Syndrome," 144, quoted in Morris, *Creation and the Modern Christian*, 71.

25. Jacques Monod, "The Secret of Life," interview with Laurie John, Australian Broadcasting Co., 10 June 1976, quoted in Morris, *The Long War Against God*, 58.

26. Furthermore, the entire evolutionary program is driven by *naturalistic* assumptions, not theistic ones. There is no point in invoking God to account for a process in which His presence is, *a priori*, not needed.

27. David Berlinski, A *Firing Line Debate*, with William F. Buckley, Jr. (Public Broadcasting System, 19 December 1997).

28. There are also many other ways to refute evolution. One subtle but very powerful approach against the atheist's version (the humanist view shared by Carl Sagan, Richard Dawkins, Stephen Jay Gould, and many other evolutionists today) involves what is called transcendental reasoning. In transcendental reasoning one must assume the thing in question in order to deny it, which shows the absurdity of denying it. In this case,

because rational humans exist, it becomes absurd to deny the existence of a personal, rational Creator. Bob and Gretchen Passantino explain that the evolutionist must believe that impersonal and "nonrational causes cause rational beings (humans with minds) who are themselves composed entirely of the nonrational, and yet are somehow able to step outside of that nonrationality and reason to the conclusion that everything is material and therefore nonrational. Yet, if the nonrational material universe is 'the whole show,' the humanist could never actually know if he is truly rational or only a nonrational material product with the illusion of rationality.

"What is more reasonable to believe, that the nonrational produces the rational; or that a rational being (God) created other rational beings (humans) and a world founded on rational principles that can therefore be understood by these rational beings? The humanist must borrow from the theistic, Christian worldview, which can account for rationality. It is ironic that humanists often accuse Christians of possessing blind faith, when Christians have justification for the scientific method, while the humanist only has blind faith that the nonrational can produce the rational. Christianity gives birth to science, while humanism only gives birth to blindness." (Bob and Gretchen Passantino, "Religion, Truth, and Value without God: Contemporary Atheism Speaks Out in Humanist Manifesto 2000," part 2. *Christian Research Journal*, 22, no. 4: 48–49, at www.equip.org/free/DR503-2.htm, accessed 29 January 2003)

STUDY GUIDE

WITH A BOOK like *Fatal Flaws*, the truest application must surely be a readiness "to give an answer to everyone who asks you" what you believe about creation and evolution. Make no mistake: if you are willing to engage the people around you, you *will* find yourself in discussions about this topic, and you *will* be called upon to make a case for why you believe what you believe.

You might think of this appendix as more of a "crib sheet" than a study guide. Here is the argument of *Fatal Flaws* boiled down to its essence. Use this guide as a way to review the book you've just finished, and you should be able to hold your own in any conversation about evolution and creation.

The evolutionary worldview has infected thought at every level in our culture; the response has to come from all of us who hold to the truth. We can't leave this battle to the scientists and the professors.

My argument is summarized by the acronym FACE—plus R, which exposes the evolutionary worldview as a FARCE. To get started, fill in the acronym below (see p. v):

F _____

A _____

C _____

E _____

+ _____

R _____

CHAPTER 1—TRUTH AND CONSEQUENCES

In this chapter, I argue that Darwin's *Origin of Species* might well be the most influential book in history, other than Scripture. The "Darwinian Revolution" has touched every area of human thought and endeavor—the intellectual, the social, the political, the interpersonal, everything. There's just one problem: Darwin's theories aren't based in fact, but metaphysical contentions and mythological tales.

1. *What is at stake in this debate?*

- The most significant consequence of evolution is that it _____ the very _____ of Christianity. (see p. 4)

- If evolution is reflective of the _____ of science, then Genesis must be reflective of the _____ of Scripture. And if the _____ of Christianity is _____, the _____ must fall. (see p. 4)

- While Bozarth predicted the demise of _____ without _____, he might just as well have predicted the demise of _____ without _____. (see p. 5)

2. *Sovereignty of Self*

- _____ was credited for expunging the need for _____. In reality, it is merely the _____ of an age-old deception. Satan promised Eve that she could become a god and decide for herself what was _____ and what was _____. (see p. 6)

- "Humanity's newfound _____ sacrificed
  _____ on the altar of _____. Ethics and
  morals were no longer determined on the basis of
  _____ _____, but rather by the size and
  strength of the latest _____ _____.
  (see p. 6–7)

3. *The Sexual Revolution*

- Instead of genuine sexual freedom, a godless,
  subjective vision of morality has given us
  _____, _____, and _____. (see p. 8)

- There is a comparison to be made between ignoring
  moral law and ignoring the law of gravity. You may
  vote unanimously to repeal the law of gravity, but
  that won't change the result should you then jump
  off a building. We can't violate God's laws without
  suffering _____, _____, and even
  _____. (see pp. 8–9)

4. *Survival of the Fittest*

- The inherently racist assumptions of evolution (e.g.,
  Darwin's belief that "lower races" of human beings
  will inevitably be eliminated by the "higher races")
  goes against the Christian teaching that in Christ there

is neither _____ nor _____, neither
_____ nor _____, neither _____ nor
_____. (see p. 10)

* The concept of evolution demands death. Death is
  as _____ to evolution as it is _____ to
  biblical creation. (see p. 11)

Chapter 2: Fossil Follies

The great secret of evolutionists is that there is *no fossil
evidence* of any transitional creature between one
species and another. In this chapter I discuss several
creatures and theories—mostly imaginary—that the
scientific community has foisted on the public as evidence of macroevolution. As we see in this chapter,
things are not always as they have been made to appear.

1. *Pseudosaurs (Archaeopteryx)*

* Archaeopteryx has long been offered as a
  transitional species between _____ and _____.
  Unfortunately, Archaeopteryx has little to tell us
  about any such transition because it was a
  _____ in the modern sense, not a transitional
  species. (see p. 19)

- Theories regarding the origins of feathers have proven to be especially fanciful. The _____ theory, for instance, holds that feathers first formed when the outer edges of the _____ of fast-running reptiles became frayed by _____ _____ acting on genetic _____. (see p. 20)

- Such myths are surely more fanciful than the idea that such an intricate design as a feather must have had a _____! (see p. 20)

2. Pro-Avis

- Equally fanciful is the myth of the pro-avis, a reptile whose frayed scales helped it catch and eat more _____, which gave it the energy to run _____, which frayed its scales even more, which eventually allowed it to _____. (see p. 23–24)

- The amount of fossil evidence (or any other evidence) for pro-avis is _____. (see p. 23)

- In the absence of evidence for classical Darwinism, evolutionists haven't become _____; they have simply become more _____. (see p. 24)

3. *Punctuated Equilibrium*

- Goldschmidt's "hopeful monster" theory is summed up in the sentence, "The first _____ hatched from a _____ egg." (see p. 25)

- Gould's theory of _____ _____ revives Goldschmidt's discredited theory. "_____" refers to long periods (millions of years) with no changes in a species. "_____" refers to rapid periods of massive change in a species. (see p. 27–28)

- Three major problems with punctuated equilibrium:

  1. It is a classic argument from _____. It is motivated by a desire to explain away the lack of _____ _____ in the fossil record. (see p. 28)

  2. It flies in the face of the science of _____. (see p. 28)

  3. The effects of "jumping genes" or chromosomal rearrangements would not produce a _____ _____, but a _____. (see p. 29)

CHAPTER 3: APE MEN — FICTION, FRAUD, AND FANTASY

Many people don't realize how much speculation — and pure imagination — goes into the images of "ape-men" that have become so familiar in the media. This chapter takes a closer look at such ape-men.

1. *Pithecanthropus Erectus (Java Man)*

- Java Man's remains consist of three _____, a _____, and a _____ —found 50 feet apart from one another! (see p. 32–33)

- Two human _____ found in close proximity to the original finds suggest that Java Man wasn't an _____ of humans after all. (see p. 33)

2. *Piltdown Man*

- Piltdown Man was "unearthed" in _____, but it wasn't until _____ that it was finally declared a fake—the jaw of an _____ intentionally stained, with its _____ filed down to resemble those of a human. (see p. 34–35)

3. *Peking Man*

- If Java Man is _____ and Piltdown Man is a _____, then Peking Man is pure _____. (see p. 36)

- Peking Man is based on a series of dubious fossil "discoveries" including some _____, fourteen _____ (all bashed in at the base), and a collection of _____. The evidence all mysteriously _____ during World War II. (pp. 36)

- In the end, researchers decided that the "Peking Man" skulls actually belonged not to ape-men, but to _____ killed by men. The tools apparently weren't used _____ Peking Man, but _____ Peking Man. (see p. 37)

- To say that "hominids" like Peking Man are related to _____ because they can both _____ upright is like saying that _____ and _____ are related because both can _____. (see p. 37–38)

CHAPTER 4: CHANCE

The idea that any part of the universe came into being by chance cannot co-exist with the idea that there is a Creator-God. But can even the most doc-trinaire evolutionists really believe that the universe came together by chance (purely natural processes)?

1. Eye

- The eye could not have developed by _____, no matter how many millions of years you allow for the process. Besides the incredible organized _____ of the eye itself, there is the fact that without the _____ development of the eye and brain in a _____ fashion, the isolated developments themselves become _____ and _____. (see p. 44)

2. Egg

- A fertilized human egg the size of a _____ contains chemical instructions that would fill more than _____ printed pages. (see p. 46)

- Statistically speaking, it would take the processes of chance _____ _____ times the assumed _____ of the earth to spell the phrase "THE THEORY OF EVOLUTION" with Scrabble tiles. (see p. 48)

- A child—that is, a being with _____ —could do the same task in _____. (see p. 48)

3. *Earth*

- Three facts from geo-sciences suggest that this planet's ability to support life is no accident:

   1. _____ is unique among liquids in that its solid state is less _____ than its liquid state. As a result, ice _____. If water were like virtually any other liquid, it would freeze from the bottom up, killing _____ life, destroying the _____ supply, and making earth _____. (see p. 49)

   2. Ocean _____ play a crucial role in our survival. If the moon were _____, higher tides would cause devastating _____ _____. If the moon were _____, tidal motion would _____, and the oceans would _____ and _____. (see p. 49)

   3. Earth's _____ is ideal for life. Closer to the sun, we would _____. Farther from the sun, we would _____. (see p. 49)

CHAPTER 5: EMPIRICAL SCIENCE

If we test the evolutionary worldview in light of the laws of science, the view doesn't fare so well.

1. Effects and Their Causes

- Common sense (as well as science) tells us that an _____ must have a _____ that is equal to or _____ than itself. (see p. 58)

- The theory of evolution attempts to make effects such as _____ _____, _____, and _____ greater than their causes— _____, _____, and _____ forces. (see p. 58)

2. Energy Conservation

- The first law of thermodynamics means that neither _____ nor _____ can appear from _____. (see p. 61)

- To put it another way, _____ comes from nothing. (see p. 62)

- The universe itself, then, could not have sprung into existence from simply nothing. (see pp. 61–62)

- Because what is living is qualitatively different than what is non-living (see p. 58), we can use the fact that the universe could not have sprung from nothing as an analogy to show that life could not have come from non-life. (see p. 62)

3. *Entropy*

- The second law of thermodynamics means that everything runs inexorably from _____ to _____ and from _____ to _____. Evolution suggests the opposite. (see p. 63)

- Evolutionists say that the theory of evolution does not violate the _____ of _____ because the constant infusion of energy from the _____ keeps earth from being a _____ system. (see p. 65)

- However, the sun's rays never produce an upswing in organized _____ without _____ (the _____ principle of life). (see p. 65)

- Energy from the sun does not produce an _____ structure of _____ without _____ and an _____. (see p. 65)

- If the sun beats down on a dead plant, it does not produce _____, but speeds up _____. (see p. 65)

CHAPTER 6: RECAPITULATION

Recapitulation is summarized by the once-popular phrase, "_____ recapitulates _____." In other words, in the course of an embryo's development, the embryo repeats the history of its species (from single-celled organism to fish to frog to tailed mammal . . .). This myth has led to serious consequences.

- In the development of a human embryo, perhaps the most familiar marker of "recapitulation" are the "_____ slits" of the "_____ stage." (see p. 70)
- These "_____ slits" are known, however, to be essential parts of human _____, not _____ vestiges. (see p. 71)

1. *Roe v. Wade*

- The "recapitulation" myth has given pro-abortionists the opportunity to claim that an early-term fetus is less

than _____ —as if killing a first-trimester fetus
were more like killing a _____ or _____
than killing a _____ _____. (see p. 72)

2. *Racism*

- Another corollary of recapitulation is the idea that
  human development—from childhood to
  _____ —recapitulates the development of the
  human race from "lower," less rational races to "
  _____," more rational and _____ races.
  (see p. 77)

3. *Theistic Evolution*

- I assert that, because it blames _____ for
  evolution, "theistic evolution" is the worst of all
  possibilities. (see p. 78)

- An _____, _____ God does not have to
  painfully plod through millions of _____,
  _____, and _____ in order to have
  fellowship with humans. Rather, He can create
  humans in a _____. If theistic evolution is true,
  Genesis is at best an _____ and at worst a
  _____. (see p. 79)

The theory of evolution is more vulnerable than its proponents would have you believe. Stand firm in the truth, and be confident in the only unassailable account of our origins: "In the beginning, God created the heavens and the earth…"